PULP

Joseph Zettelmaier

BROADWAY PLAY PUBLISHING INC
New York
www.broadwayplaypub.com
info@broadwayplaypub.com

I0139610

Cover art by Sarah Beth Hall, courtesy of Know Theatre

First edition: April 2018
I S B N: 978-0-88145-767-4

Book design: Marie Donovan
Page make-up: Adobe InDesign
Typeface: Palatino

PULP was performed as a Rolling World Premiere with the National New Play Network.

The first production opened at the Phoenix Theatre in Indianapolis on 11 February 2016 with the following cast and creative contributors:

FRANK.. Eric Olson
DESIREE..Angela Plank
BRADLEY..Josh Coomer
LYNCROFT... Ian Cruz
WALTER..Michael Hosp

Director..Bryan Fonseca
Set design...................................... Bernie Killian
Lighting design ....Jeffery Martin
Costume & prop design ....Emily McGee
Sound design...................................... Tom Horan
Stage manager............................Chelsey Stauffer

PULP opened at Williamston Theatre in Williamston, MI, on 22 September 2016 with the following cast and creative contributors:

FRANK...John Lepard
DESIREE...Alysia Kolascz
BRADLEY...Aral Gribble
LYNCROFT...Mark Colson
WALTER .... Joe Bailey

Director..Tony Caselli
Set design .... Matt Imhoff
Lighting design ....Shannon Schweitzer
Costume design ....Elspeth Williams
Sound design... Julia Garlotte
Props design .... Michelle Raymond
Stage manager..Stefanie Din

PULP opened at the KNOW Theatre in Cincinnati on 7 October 2016 with the following cast and creative contributors:

FRANK .... Paul Riopelle
DESIREE .... Maggie Lou Rader
BRADLEY .... Darnell Pierre Benjamin
LYNCROFT .... Dylan Shelton
WALTER .... Justin McCombs

Director .... Andrew Hungerford
Set design .... Sarah Beth Hall
Lighting design .... Andrew Hungerford
Costume design .... Noelle Wedig
Sound & projection design .... Douglas Borntrager
Stage manager .... Emily Elizabeth James

CHARACTERS & SETTING

FRANK ELLERY, *a private detective*
DESIREE ST CLAIR, *a pulp writer (romance)*
BRADLEY RAYBURN, *a pulp writer (science fiction)*
WALTER KINGSTON-SMITH, *a pulp writer (hero pulps)*
R A LYNCROFT, *a pulp writer (horror)*

Time: Spring 1933
Place: Los Angeles, California

ACT ONE

Scene 1

(Lights up. A detective's office in the 1930s. It is dirty, disorganized and unoccupied. A voiceover is heard.)

FRANK: *(V O)* You live in the city long enough, you think there are no surprises left. Here, there's room for all seven of the deadly sins, plus a few more for good measure. I've seen the devil in a three-piece suit with an angel on each arm; I've seen a dead man light up a Chesterfield and a bum with a heart of gold and teeth to match. Yeah, this city is rotten to the core. Rotten and filthy and full of maggots that...

(The sound of vomiting. FRANK staggers out of the bathroom.)

FRANK: *(V O)* That's me. Frank Ellery, P I. And I used to be just like you. A bright-eyed kid with dreams. Look at me now.

(FRANK downs a shot of whiskey and belches. He is not wearing pants.)

FRANK: *(V O)* The city feeds on dreams. Gobbles them up like a fat man at Thanksgiving dinner. That's how I ended up in this rat-trap office, no secretary, no money, and no prospects. I'd spent too many years taking the cases even the lowest rat wouldn't touch. Why? Because I was even lower. Cheating husbands, blackmail, dope fiends. You need a rotten job done on the cheap? Frank Ellery's your man. I'd all but given up on everything. Until she walked in the door.

(DESIREE *enters. She is a beautiful woman in her 30s, dressed very well.*)

FRANK: *(V O)* A dame is the kind of woman you have fun with, but you don't take home to mother. A broad…she'll laugh with the fellas, talk like the fellas and crack you in the jaw when your hands start to wander. But the woman who walked through my door that rainy Friday morning…she was a lady.

DESIREE: Are you Mr Ellery?

FRANK: Well, I sure as hell ain't his sister.

(Beat)

DESIREE: All right then. My name is Desiree St Claire. Have you heard of me?

FRANK: Can't say that I…

DESIREE: It's of no consequence. If you are in fact Mr Frank Ellery, I would like to discuss hiring you for a job, or a case or whatever you call it.

FRANK: Can ya gimme two seconds with the Listerine first?

DESIREE: Mr Ellery, I can give you entire minutes.

FRANK: Hot damn.

(FRANK *staggers into the bathroom. The sound of gargling.* DESIREE *walks around the room.*)

DESIREE: This is quite a place you have here.

(FRANK *spits in the sink.*)

DESIREE: Have you ever thought of hiring someone to clean it now and then?

FRANK: Lady, this is the cleanest it's been in months.

DESIREE: I see.

(The sound of water running in the sink.)

DESIREE: Do you mind if I smoke?

FRANK: I'd mind more if you didn't.

(DESIREE takes a cigarette from his pack and lights it up.)

DESIREE: So you prefer Old Golds?

FRANK: You smokin' my cigarettes?

DESIREE: I am. And you didn't answer my question.

FRANK: I figured it was rhetorical.

DESIREE: I am many things, Mr Ellery, but rhetorical isn't one of them.

(FRANK comes out of the bathroom, wiping his face with a towel.)

FRANK: Yeah, I smoke 'em. Probably as close as I'll ever get to real gold.

DESIREE: You have a sense of humor. I like that.

FRANK: Swell.

DESIREE: I have no patience for people without one.

FRANK: "I laugh because I must not cry." Lincoln said that.

DESIREE: That is all. That is all.

FRANK: I guess. I wasn't there when he said it.

DESIREE: No, Mr Ellery. That is the full quote. "I laugh because I must not cry. That is all. That is all." *(Beat)* I feel that we're at the point in the conversation where you must either put pants on or I must take something off.

(Beat. FRANK finds some pants, begins dressing.)

FRANK: So you want to hire me or something?

DESIREE: Yes. Indeed I do.

FRANK: Twenty dollars a day, plus expenses.

DESIREE: What kind of expenses?

FRANK: I don't know. You haven't told me what you want yet.

DESIREE: Fair enough. I would like you to investigate a murder.

FRANK: They got cops for that.

DESIREE: I trust the local constabulary as far as you could throw them.

FRANK: I think that's as far as *you* could throw them.

DESIREE: Oh, Mr Ellery. I have muscles you can't even imagine. *(Beat)* Besides, I believe you have a very specific insight to this matter that the police do not.

FRANK: I'm listening.

DESIREE: Bernard Wolcott has been murdered.

(Beat)

FRANK: Come again.

DESIREE: Not on a first date.

FRANK: What?

DESIREE: A joke, Mr Ellery. If you truly didn't hear me, I said, "Bernard Wolcott has been murdered". Shall I repeat myself again or are we all caught up?

FRANK: Someone killed Bernie Wolcott?

DESIREE: And we are on the same page. Yes, murdered in a most gruesome manner.

FRANK: How?

DESIREE: Will you accept the case?

FRANK: Details first.

DESIREE: Bernard was found this morning in his townhouse. He hadn't shown up for a meeting with one of his clients. When said client arrived at his place of residence, they found him in his bedroom, dead as the proverbial doornail.

FRANK: I'm waiting to hear the gruesome part.

DESIREE: His heart had been removed from his chest. Brutally. Savagely.

FRANK: Jesus Christ.

DESIREE: The police arrived on the scene shortly thereafter. Appropriately enough, they said his upper torso had been "pulped."

FRANK: What do you mean?

DESIREE: It was a play on words. As you know, Bernard was a literary agent for several writers who…

FRANK: I know what he did. I want to know what the police were talking about.

DESIREE: Ah. Of course. Someone had cut open his chest, cracked his ribcage like a lobster shell, and ripped out his heart. The process was far from surgical, if you take my meaning.

FRANK: Brutal. Savage.

DESIREE: Precisely.

FRANK: And you're sure it wasn't natural causes.

(DESIREE *laughs.*)

DESIREE: I was told you had a singular wit.

FRANK: Says who?

DESIREE: Oh, you're not unknown in certain circles.

FRANK: What circles are those?

DESIREE: Haven't you guessed it? I was one of Bernard's clients.

FRANK: You don't say.

DESIREE: I do say. Although I doubt very much that you're familiar with my work.

FRANK: Try me. I'm more literate than I look.

DESIREE: I've mostly been published in Fantastic Romance, Avon and the like.

FRANK: You're a pulp writer.

DESIREE: Romance novelist, yes.

FRANK: I don't read romance. Hell, I don't even live romance.

DESIREE: Oh, I find that hard to believe. *(Beat)* Needless to say, I was crushed by Bernie's passing.

FRANK: You said he died this morning.

DESIREE: Yes.

FRANK: You recovered fast.

(DESIREE leans in very close to FRANK's face.)

DESIREE: Can't you see the tears? *(Beat)* So do we have a deal?

FRANK: Who found the body?

DESIREE: Excuse me?

FRANK: Before I spit-n-shake, I need to know the facts. Who found Bernie?

DESIREE: Bradley Rayburn.

FRANK: Outer space guy.

DESIREE: Insomuch as he writes science fiction, not that he's actually from outer space.

FRANK: Right. Can you get me a list of Bernie's clients?

(DESIREE removes a piece of paper from her purse.)

FRANK: There's only four names on this list. Including yours.

DESIREE: Dear Bernard had run on hard times. We were the only writers loyal enough to stay aboard the sinking ship.

FRANK: I'd heard Bernie was circling the drain. I gotta tell you right off, this looks fishy.

DESIREE: How so?

FRANK: I knew Bernie well enough. No wife, no kids and no enemies. Who'd want to do this to him?

DESIREE: Well, that is what I'm hiring you to find out.

FRANK: The cops name you as a suspect?

(Beat)

DESIREE: Why on earth would they do that?

FRANK: Yes or no.

DESIREE: Yes.

FRANK: So am I here to solve this crime, or to prove you didn't do it?

DESIREE: It is my deepest, sincerest hope that the two are not mutually exclusive. Mr Ellery, may I speak frankly?

FRANK: Why not?

DESIREE: I know who you are. I know what's happened to you.

FRANK: You got no idea…

DESIREE: And I know that you are feeling the financial pinch. Take the job, Mr Ellery, and I'll see to it that you receive all that's coming to you and more.

FRANK: Fancy duds don't necessarily make a rich dame.

DESIREE: In this instance, appearances are not deceiving.

FRANK: Hmm.

DESIREE: So do we have a deal?

(*Beat.* FRANK *thinks about it, then offers* DESIREE *his hand. She stares at it.*)

FRANK: Don't worry. I don't spit.

(DESIREE *smiles, takes it, and steps in close.*)

DESIREE: Neither do I.

FRANK: Oh. I…um…

DESIREE: Do you have a pen?

FRANK: Probably.

(DESIREE *searches a desk, removes a sterling silver pen.*)

DESIREE: This will do. (*She writes down her number.*) I can be reached at this number. Please keep me abreast of the situation, Mr Ellery.

FRANK: Frank. You can call me Frank.

DESIREE: And you can call me…anytime.

(DESIREE *exits.* FRANK *sits, pocketing the money and staring at the card.*)

(*Lights fade.*)

Scene 2

(*The voiceover is heard as the scene changes.*)

FRANK: (*V O*) The next day, a few cops got greasy palms and I got a copy of the police report. It was just like Ms St Clair had said. The body was found at nine in the morning by Bradley Rayburn. Bernie had been mutilated, but there was no sign of forced entry, no fingerprints, no murder weapon. The cops were at a loss, and at that point, so was I. Normally they wouldn't give two bits for a down on-his-luck bookworm, but the way it was done…that was weird enough to warrant some attention. They pursued their leads, I pursued mine. I knew Bradley Rayburn. Knew his work, anyway. He was a fresh face, an up-and-comer. Amazing Stories and Galaxy Science Fiction. *Beyond Saturn, Fishing in the Sea of Tranquility, Blorgs from the Lost Planet*…he wrote 'em all. That's not to say he was rich. Or famous. He was a pulp writer. A good one, but still a dime a dozen. Overworked, underpaid, typing his fingers bloody trying to make the deadline. It's a damn shame when an imagination like his has to sing and dance for a buck, but until Bradley's vision of the future came true, he had to schlep it like the rest of us.

(BRADLEY RAYBURN's place. It is a clutter of papers, a globe, a telescope, various scientific accoutrements and a typewriter. He is typing away madly. He is in his early twenties, wearing a rumpled suit and glasses. He is a nervous, twitchy man. A knock on the door. He stops typing, remains silent. A knock again)

BRADLEY: Go away!

FRANK: Mr Rayburn, my name's Frank Ellery. Can I have a word?

BRADLEY: You just had eleven. Twelve if you don't count contractions. Now get lost!

FRANK: It won't take long.

BRADLEY: Amscray, flatfoot! I'm done talking!

FRANK: I'm not a policeman, Mr Rayburn.

(BRADLEY checks to make sure the door chain is latched, then opens the door a little.)

BRADLEY: I am a very busy man! I have to get this story done tonight, so whatever…

(FRANK quickly reaches through, grabbing BRADLEY by the throat.)

FRANK: Look, pal. I'm playing as nice as I can here. I got a couple questions to ask, and I'll be outta your hair. So open this door before I kick it down.

BRADLEY: I have...a...door chain...

FRANK: And I got ten years experience kicking down doors. Wanna see which one wins out?

(FRANK *releases* BRADLEY, *who slams the door shut.*)

FRANK: I don't hear unlocking.

BRADLEY: I have a gun!

FRANK: No you don't. But I have a size twelve boot that's looking for something to do.

(BRADLEY *paces in a panic.*)

FRANK: One...two...

(BRADLEY *opens the door.*)

BRADLEY: Well come in already, you barbarian.

FRANK: Barbarian? I like that.

(FRANK *enters, handing* BRADLEY *a card.*)

FRANK: Like I said, name's Ellery. I'm a P I, fully licensed by the state. I'm gonna ask you a few questions, you're gonna gimme a few answers. Square?

BRADLEY: Square, triangle, octagon, whichever you want. Just get on with it.

(FRANK *walks around the room.*)

FRANK: Nice place you got here.

BRADLEY: You think so?

FRANK: No. (*He starts looking through a stack of papers.*)

BRADLEY: No. No no no no no. Put that down.

FRANK: New story?

BRADLEY: Yes. Put it down.

(FRANK *reads the title.*)

FRANK: *The Blorg Giveth, The Blorg Taketh Away.* Hey! Another Blorg story?

BRADLEY: Yes, I…you know what a Blorg is?

FRANK: Sure, sure. Big talking space bird. Everyone thought they were here to attack us, but turns out they just wanted to trade their technology for our….shit, what was it?

BRADLEY: Soy beans.

FRANK: Right! Or else they'd die or something.

BRADLEY: Soy beans contain an enzyme they can't produce on their own, and the vegetation on their planet was dying off so…

FRANK: They thought Earth was a market.

BRADLEY: It was an indictment of consumerism. I can't believe you read that one.

FRANK: Good story. Nice mix of humor and…you know, big words.

BRADLEY: Oh. Um…thank you.

(*As* FRANK *walks, he spins the globe, which clearly makes* BRADLEY *uncomfortable.*)

FRANK: So I wanna ask you about Bernie Wolcott.

BRADLEY: I was with the police all day yesterday. I told them everything.

FRANK: Then this should be pretty easy. You found him…?

BRADLEY: Yesterday morning. Six o'clock.

FRANK: How's that?

BRADLEY: How's what?

FRANK: Police report had you calling them at nine o'clock.

BRADLEY: That's what I said. Nine o'clock.

FRANK: You said six o'clock.

BRADLEY: I think you're wrong.

FRANK: I know what you said.

BRADLEY: So do I, and since I'm the one who said it, I think I'm most likely right, Mr Man!

(Beat)

BRADLEY: I'm sorry. I don't mean to be so…

FRANK: It's all right.

BRADLEY: Would you mind if I poured myself a drink?

FRANK: Pour away.

(BRADLEY goes to the kitchen.)

BRADLEY: Would you like a drink?

FRANK: Love one. But I'm on the job, so…

BRADLEY: Of course. You're a man who clings to his own moral code like a dog to a mailman's keister.

FRANK: You could say that.

BRADLEY: I could and I did. *(He returns with a glass of wine.)*

(BRADLEY sits, motions FRANK to do the same.)

BRADLEY: I'm sorry for before. I'm still pretty rattled.

FRANK: Sure.

BRADLEY: I want whoever did this caught. Not in a year, not in ten years. Now.

FRANK: Believe me, pal. That's what I want too. So look…I know from deadlines. I'm not here to give you a nosebleed. I'm just gonna ask a few questions, and I'm gone.

BRADLEY: All right.

FRANK: All right. How would you describe your relationship with Wolcott?

BRADLEY: What do you mean?

FRANK: Were you just work colleagues or…?

BRADLEY: Friends. We were friends.

FRANK: Did he have a lot of friends?

BRADLEY: Honestly?

FRANK: No. I'd love it if you lied to me.

BRADLEY: He didn't have many friends. Bernie was… he gave most people a rash. If he wanted something from you, he was relentless. Annoyingly so.

FRANK: Why four?

BRADLEY: Four what? Seasons?

FRANK: Clients. My sources tell me you were one of just four.

BRADLEY: Like I said, most people couldn't handle Bernie for more than five minutes.

FRANK: But you're not most people.

BRADLEY: He believed in me, in my work, before anyone else ever did. He truly thought I had something…a gift. I'm not…I've been kicked around a lot in this life, Mr Ellery. I've found a little kindness can go a long way.

(FRANK *smiles*.)

BRADLEY: You think that's funny?

FRANK: No, just…I met Bernie. A couple times in fact.

BRADLEY: Really?

FRANK: Yeah, years ago. Another life. Obnoxious as all hell, like you said. But…yeah, somethin' about him.

BRADLEY: An easy man to mock, but a hard man to hate.

FRANK: Somethin' like that.

BRADLEY: Is that why you're investigating this? For Bernie, I mean.

FRANK: Do I look like I do pro bono? Some dame hired me.

BRADLEY: Heh. I didn't realize Bernie knew any women…oh. Desiree. Of course.

FRANK: Of course?

BRADLEY: She knows she's the number one suspect, so why not put on a little song and dance, play the grieving….

FRANK: Romance writer?

BRADLEY: …and throw everyone off the scent.

FRANK: You think she did it?

BRADLEY: I think she could've done it, sure.

FRANK: So Bernie did have enemies.

(Beat)

BRADLEY: I didn't say that.

FRANK: You kinda did.

BRADLEY: No. No no no. That's not…you're grilling me!

FRANK: Calm down.

BRADLEY: You think…I'm not going to incriminate…I haven't done anything wrong!

FRANK: No one said you did.

(BRADLEY *starts having trouble breathing.*)

FRANK: Hey! Hey! Relax!

BRADLEY: Oh god…oh god…

FRANK: You want I should call a doctor?

BRADLEY: No…just give me…wait…

(BRADLEY *runs into another room, slamming the door.*
FRANK *goes to it, finds it locked.*)

FRANK: C'mon, Rayburn! We've danced this number already!

(*No response*)

FRANK: Don't make me kick this one down. 'Cause I'll do it! (*He shakes the door hard, trying to get it open.*) One! Two!… (*Beat*) Two! (*Beat*) TWO!

(*Still no response*)

FRANK: Ah, the hell with this…

(FRANK *is about to kick the door when it swings open.*
BRADLEY *is standing there with a strange looking apparatus on his chest and head. It has a distinctly Thirties Sci-Fi look, complete with a bowl over his head.*)

FRANK: Sweet Christmas!

(FRANK *almost falls over, staggering away from* BRADLEY.)

BRADLEY: Just give me a minute, Mr Ellery.

FRANK: What the hell are you wearing?

BRADLEY: A device of my own design. Nothing to be scared of, really.

(BRADLEY *motions for* FRANK *to sit.* FRANK *just stares at him.*)

BRADLEY: Well, I'm sitting whether you want to or not.

(BRADLEY *sits, takes his glass of wine. He tries to sip, but forgets he's wearing a glass helmet.*)

BRADLEY: Ah, dammit. (*He sets the glass down.*)

BRADLEY: I have asthma, Mr Ellery. Very severe athsma. When I get overly excited, I have difficulty breathing. This… *(He taps his helmet.)* …delivers pure oxygen to my faulty lungs, and helps me…come to sorts.

FRANK: You built that?

BRADLEY: I did.

FRANK: You must be some kind of genius or something.

BRADLEY: I wouldn't go that far. I'm an inventor. A tinkerer. I found that the more I wrote science fiction, the more I wondered how much of it might be possible in the here and now. This was one of my successes.

FRANK: I'm almost scared to ask about your failures.

BRADLEY: They weren't pretty.

(A chime goes off.)

BRADLEY: Ah! *(He removes his helmet.)* There we are. Perfectly oxygenated. That's much better.

FRANK: I've never seen anything like this.

BRADLEY: We live in a world of wonders, Frank. May I call you "Frank?"

(FRANK nods.)

BRADLEY: I spend every hour of every day thinking about what the world will be like ten years from now… twenty, fifty, a hundred. These things I write…they pay the bills, sure, but what I really want is for people to read them and think "You know what? I'd really like a flying car. How would one go about building that?"

FRANK: Did…did you try?

BRADLEY: It wasn't pretty.

(As FRANK examines the helmet, BRADLEY looks at his notebook.)

BRADLEY: My god, your handwriting is awful.

FRANK: Hey!

BRADLEY: Like a spastic monkey with a pencil.

(FRANK *grabs* BRADLEY *roughly.*)

FRANK: Drop it, spaceman.

(FRANK *takes the book back.*)

BRADLEY: Listen, I understand why you came to me, but I'm a dead end. I don't know anything.

FRANK: Everyone knows something, whether they know it or not.

(Beat)

BRADLEY: All right then.

FRANK: Someone out there wanted Bernie Wolcott dead, and I'm getting paid to find out who. Best way to do that is to find out why.

BRADLEY: Motive.

FRANK: Motive.

BRADLEY: So…then you would need to talk to his four clients.

FRANK: Why would I do that?

BRADLEY: We're the ones who knew him best.

FRANK: He must've had a sweetheart or a favorite aunt or…

BRADLEY: No. The four of us were basically his entire life.

(Beat. FRANK *smiles.* BRADLEY *catches on.)*

BRADLEY: You're good.

FRANK: I get by.

BRADLEY: Well, I can save you some time. You want to meet all of us? Get a nice suit and cancel your plans tomorrow night. Assuming you have any.

FRANK: Suits?

BRADLEY: Plans.

FRANK: Why?

BRADLEY: There's an event. Lyncroft is doing a reading from his newest story. Small invited group, and I'm one of the invited.

FRANK: R A Lyncroft. He's one of the four.

BRADLEY: You know him?

FRANK: Sorta.

BRADLEY: Well, Desiree and Walter will almost certainly be there.

FRANK: And what am I? Your date?

BRADLEY: Sorry, big boy. We're from two different worlds.

(Lights change.)

Scene 3

(Voiceover as the scene changes.)

FRANK: *(V O)* Did I know R A Lyncroft? Sure. Anyone who ever picked up a copy of Weird Tales knew his name. He was their number one draw, the undisputed master of horror. Critics hated him, but that didn't hurt his sales any. The thing about Lyncroft is…he didn't go for the traditional scares. No ghosts, no boogeymen under the bed. Nah, his stuff was more…disturbed. He'd created this entire mythology based around these ancient demonic things, gods of the world that existed before this one. And not kind gods. All they wanted to was to take this world back. Whatever sick thing lived in the back of Lyncroft's mind, he'd turned it into greenbacks. Yeah, the guy gave me chills…and not just 'cause of his stories.

*(Lights rise. It is later that night, a small gathering.
LYNCROFT stands behind a podium, reading the final part of
his novella. He is a severe, humorless man.)*

LYNCROFT: "And so I have descended into the caves,
led only by the ramblings of poor Marcus, now
hopelessly insane. I crawl through the tunnels, ever
deeper into the primeval abyss, with but one goal.
I must discover the ancient tomb of Zal'n-thok, the
slumbering deity, the mad-god of the world before this
world. For tho' he yet sleeps, he invades the minds of
his scattered faithful…whispering his dread secrets
in their dreams. I know now that Marcus was one of
them, and perhaps I am as well. Zal'n-thok prepares us
for his return; for when the cosmos aligns and the first
ones rise again. Somewhere within this dark expanse,
he waits. I do not know how long I've been beneath
the earth. Weeks? Months? Time means nothing in the
stillness with no sun. On occasion, I feel a wind rise
around me…a cold air deeper than any surface storm
could reach. It is his breath…the breath of Zal'n-thok.
My own sanity balks at his name, for I am certain not
only that he lives…but that soon, the Sleeper shall
awaken."

*(He closes his notebook. The audience applauds. He nods and
exits. Lights rise on WALTER and DESIREE. WALTER is a
handsome, well-dressed man in his 30s-40s.)*

WALTER: Gosh, that was just…gosh.

DESIREE: Good old Lyncroft. Always leaves you
wanting more…morphine.

WALTER: Well, I thought it was a real corker. When the
narrator goes to visit his friend at the asylum, only to
find an empty straight-jacket covered in viscera…

DESIREE: I was there when he read it, Walter.

WALTER: Gave me the goosepimples, and I'm not ashamed to admit it.

DESIREE: Oh, I've always found a little shame makes life more interesting.

(WALTER *laughs.*)

WALTER: I've said it before, and I'll say it again; You, Desiree, have a wicked tongue.

DESIREE: Aren't you a dear?

WALTER: Oh! Speaking of "deer", I must tell you about my latest safari!

DESIREE: No, no. That's quite all right. I…

WALTER: There I was, in the savannah with nothing but my Model 65 and Tup-Tup, my Punjabi guide. We were hunting the elusive Western Hartebeest …

(BRADLEY *enters with* FRANK.)

DESIREE: Bradley! Darling!

BRADLEY: Des!

(BRADLEY *and* DESIREE *kiss on the cheek.*)

WALTER: Bradley, old boy! I was hoping you were here! I was just telling Desiree…

DESIREE: The only man I know who doesn't swoon at my kiss!

BRADLEY: Really, Des.

DESIREE: Sweetie, teasing is how I show my affection. So what brings you to our little gathering?

FRANK: All four of you in one room. That's what brung me.

DESIREE: Have you met Walter? Detective Frank Ellery, meet Walter Kingston-Smith.

(FRANK *and* WALTER *shake hands.*)

WALTER: A pleasure, officer.

FRANK: I'm a P I, actually.

WALTER: Oh! A bloodhound!

FRANK: Yep.

WALTER: A bird dog!

FRANK: Yep.

WALTER: A dick!

DESIREE: And I see you've already met Bradley.

BRADLEY: He gave me quite the shakedown.

DESIREE: I'm sure you hated that.

WALTER: You must be the fellow that Desiree hired! You know, to solve this unfortunate business with poor Bernie.

FRANK: That's me.

WALTER: Well, do you have any suspects yet?

FRANK: I'm lookin' at three of 'em right now.

(Beat)

WALTER: You can't possibly think one of us did it.

FRANK: Buddy boy, you'd be amazed at the things I can think of.

WALTER: But…but I'm not a killer! I'm a writer!

FRANK: Yeah, I know. You write them hero pulps…. The guy in the long cape, runs around at night, solving crimes, taking down corrupt cops…the guy with the mask…The…Masked Cape?

WALTER: The Cloak.

FRANK: The Cloak! That's it! So how's the writing going, Walt?

WALTER: Ah…well, actually. Quite well.

FRANK: So I hear. Little bird tells me the CBS is gonna turn it into a radio show.

(Beat. WALTER is shocked.)

FRANK: Did I misspeak? Ain't that public knowledge?

WALTER: It's certainly more public now.

BRADLEY: Really?! Walter, that's wonderful!

WALTER: Oh, ah….thank you, Bradley. Nothing official yet. The wheels are just now spinning into motion.

FRANK: Oh yeah? Why's that?

(DESIREE gives a false laugh at some unheard conversation. They stare at her.)

DESIREE: Well, I'm sorry, but how long were you going to go without paying attention to me?

FRANK: I was just askin' a few questions is all.

DESIREE: Yes, yes and that's all well and good. But this is a party, for god's sake.

(LYNCROFT enters.)

LYNCROFT: Yes. And glad I am that you were all in attendance.

WALTER: Linny, old man! Well done! Well done!

(WALTER shakes LYNCROFT's hand vigorously. LYNCROFT is uncomfortable.)

LYNCROFT: Yes. That's quite enough.

WALTER: A ripping good tale! Just ripping!

DESIREE: Where you come up with that morbid stuff is beyond me.

BRADLEY: I did have a thought. Why did you have the narrator go underground? Wouldn't it be more dramatic if he…

LYNCROFT: Did I ask?

(An uncomfortable silence)

LYNCROFT: And who might you be?

FRANK: Frank Ellery, P I.

(FRANK offers his hand. LYNCROFT stares at it.)

FRANK: Don't worry. I don't spit.

LYNCROFT: Why on earth would you?

FRANK: I…I mean…

LYNCROFT: Do you enjoy the macabre, Mr Ellery?

FRANK: Huh?

LYNCROFT: Horror. Terror. Penny Dreadfuls. The genre in which I write.

FRANK: Oh. Uh, yeah, actually I do.

LYNCROFT: Then what did you think of my reading? *(Beat. He looks at his colleagues.)* That is what a solicited opinion looks like. Remember it.

FRANK: O K. I like the way you draw this parallel between the narrator and his pal Marcus. In the beginning, we got the Narrator looking down at him, thinking "Jesus, my poor weak friend went nuts." And then as the story goes, we see the exact same thing happen to him. It leaves this impression that…if the things he experienced happened to any of us, then we'd all go bonkers too, you know?

LYNCROFT: Crude vernacular aside, that is a skillful review of my work.

BRADLEY: If you'd let me finish, I was going to say something similar.

LYNCROFT: But you didn't.

DESIREE: Mr Ellery is investigating the murder of…

LYNCROFT: …Bernard Wolcott. That much is obvious.

WALTER: It is?

LYNCROFT: But if I am to be investigated, I would like to know who I'm dealing with.

FRANK: Not gonna lie, that sounds like a guilty man talking.

LYNCROFT: Believe me when I say you have no conception of the kind of…man I am.

(Beat)

WALTER: I wonder if the wait staff has any more of those little quiches…

BRADLEY: I should've mentioned that Lyncroft can be a bit intense.

FRANK: We actually met before.

LYNCROFT: Did we?

FRANK: Fifteen years ago.

LYNCROFT: Ah. Early in my career. Those days are all but lost to me, sir. My mind is occupied with more cosmic matters.

FRANK: You were an odd duck them, but you're a lot odder now.

(LYNCROFT smiles a little bit.)

LYNCROFT: You are not without insight, Mr Ellery. And you are also a man of books. Do I assess that correctly?

FRANK: Yep.

LYNCROFT: You chose well, Ms St Clair. This man may have what it takes to untie this knot.

FRANK: Sounds like you already know what happened.

LYNCROFT: By no means. It will make observing you all the more interesting.

FRANK: You're a suspect. You get that, right?

LYNCROFT: Of course. A fly can best observe the spider from within its web.

WALTER: Oh, that's good! Let me just… *(He pulls out a notepad and writes.)*

FRANK: You're all suspects. The four of you. We clear on that?

DESIREE: Of course.

BRADLEY: Sure.

WALTER: "…from within its web…"

LYNCROFT: You may call on me tomorrow, if you'd like. I'll answer whatever questions you pose.

FRANK: I may just do that.

LYNCROFT: Then I bid you good evening. *(He leaves.)*

BRADLEY: Why do we keep going to these readings? The man's an ass.

WALTER: And more successful than the three of us put together.

DESIREE: Says the soon-to-be Star of the Airwaves.

WALTER: Now don't…that's still hush-hush. So Mr Ellery, have you made any deductions yet?

FRANK: Maybe.

WALTER: Please feel free to compare notes with me. You're in my genre, after all.

FRANK: Yeah?

WALTER: Strange murders, colorful suspects, and a man fighting for his own sense of justice. I imagine you've been to the scene of the crime?

FRANK: Lemme tell you how this works, moustache. I get information, I don't give it away.

WALTER: Oh! Very good! Very, very good…let me… *(He writes in his notepad.)* "…I don't…give it…" *(He sees an unseen waiter.)* Ah! The quiche! *(He walks off.)*

FRANK: Hey! I got a couple questions…

BRADLEY: Don't worry. Walter's not hard to track down. Galavanting playboy to a tee.

DESIREE: Simple as Simon going to the fair.

BRADLEY: Oh, he's not so bad, for a silver spoon.

DESIREE: I heard he's…

BRADLEY: He's not.

DESIREE: You're sure?

BRADLEY: Darling, I can always tell.

(BRADLEY *and* DESIREE *laugh.*)

FRANK: You two seem awful chummy.

DESIREE: Brad and I adore each other! Don't we?

BRADLEY: Thick as thieves. Bernie introduced us… when was it?

DESIREE: Two years ago. That romp at the Cicada Club.

BRADLEY: Oh god! Yes! I had gotten utterly boiled on gin and…

DESIREE: Poor boy spent ten minutes flirting with a coat rack.

BRADLEY: I never! Anyway, this angel came down from heaven…

DESIREE: Ha!

BRADLEY: And walked me home. We spent all night just kibitzing like long lost chums.

DESIREE: The advantage of not writing in the same milieu.

BRADLEY: But behind each other's back? The claws come out.

(BRADLEY *and* DESIREE *laugh again.*)

DESIREE: Bradley dear, would you be a lamb and fetch my coat and purse? I'd like a moment with our strapping detective.

BRADLEY: Of course, sweetie.

DESIREE: Darling.

BRADLEY: Cupcake.

DESIREE: Precious.

(BRADLEY *exits.* DESIREE *grabs* FRANK.)

DESIREE: I'm scared, Frank. Scared for my life.

FRANK: What? Why?

DESIREE: I'm being followed. I'm sure of it.

FRANK: You seen someone?

DESIREE: The corner of my eye. Every time I turn, he's gone.

FRANK: Can you describe him?

DESIREE: Black suit, wide brimmed hat…a long coat.

FRANK: Sounds like he's trying to keep his face hid.

DESIREE: What if Bernie was just the first, Frank? What if I'm next?

FRANK: Don't worry, Doll. I'm on the scent, and this dog don't stop til he catches the fox.

(DESIREE *embraces* FRANK.)

DESIREE: Oh thank you, Frank. Thank you.

FRANK: Careful. You don't want people to talk.

DESIREE: Let them talk. I don't care. I feel safe with you.

(FRANK *lifts* DESIREE's *chin with his fingers.*)

FRANK: Miss St Claire, I'm a lot of things, but safe ain't one of 'em.

(*Lights fade.*)

Scene 4

(Voiceover as the scene changes.)

FRANK: *(V O)* This case was getting more interesting by the day. I'd met my four suspects, and my gut was telling me that one of 'em did it. Sure, there was a chance it was just some nutcase, a random act of a stranger, but I didn't think so. Bernie's place hadn't been broken into, which means either the killer had a key, or Bernie let them in. Either way, it seemed like someone the poor stiff knew. Next step was to figure out the why. No one takes the time to mess up a body like that without good reason." So I spent the next day collecting all the pulps I could get my hands on, so long as one of the suspects wrote in 'em. And that night, I took R A Lyncroft up on his offer.

(LYNCROFT's parlor. It is dark, run-down and eerie. Lit by candles. FRANK ambles around, taking it in.)

FRANK: C'mon, Lyncroft. I ain't got all night.

(LYNCROFT enters, covered in what looks to be blood. FRANK draws his pistol.)

FRANK: Christ! What is this?

LYNCROFT: Paint, Mr Ellery.

FRANK: What?

LYNCROFT: I'm assuming you're assuming I'm covered in blood, when in fact it's crimson paint.

(He retrieves a fresh painting. It is quite good, depicting a man being attacked by strange, tentacled things.)

LYNCROFT: I have a guest arriving shortly. Someone who appreciates my artwork. I thought you might like this too. Do you, Mr Ellery? Do you like it?

FRANK: I, uh… Jeez, this is pretty good.

LYNCROFT: Yes. It came to me last night, in a dream.

FRANK: This is what you dream about?

(Beat)

LYNCROFT: I remember you, Mr Ellery.

FRANK: Huh?

LYNCROFT: From when we met, all those years ago. Are you not the same Francis Ellery who illustrated the first issue of *Strange Tales* I was published in?

(Beat)

FRANK: Like you said, those days are lost.

LYNCROFT: Never lost, sir. If I recall, my story was the basis for your illustration.

FRANK: *The Eldritch Horror.*

LYNCROFT: Indeed. A remarkable work, wouldn't you agree?

FRANK: I thought you weren't interested in opinions.

LYNCROFT: Generally not. As they say, everyone's a critic. Of course a critic is nothing more than a false prophet, a speck whose opinion has been elevated above others for no good reason.

FRANK: Sounds like you don't love them any more than they love you.

LYNCROFT: Whatever friends or strangers say of my work, it sells. And sells very well. Emotion is the key. All human beings feel, Mr Ellery, and fear…there is no stronger, more primal emotion than fear.

FRANK: So did you kill Bernard Wolcott?

LYNCROFT: If I said "no", would you believe me?

FRANK: Just thought I'd ask.

LYNCROFT: I have my suspicions, of course. But…

FRANK: But what?

(LYNCROFT *suddenly grabs* FRANK.)

LYNCROFT: Bernard Wolcott was a peddler, nothing more. A salesman for the grand creators. He was a slave to forces greater than anything he could imagine…greater than any could imagine, save me.

(The shadows begin to dance on the walls, taking strange shapes.)

LYNCROFT: They whisper beyond the doorway. The First Ones. The gods of old, creatures that work their will through me. Can you not see them, sir? You captured them so fully in your art.

FRANK: That was just a picture, something I drew 'cause of what you wrote!

LYNCROFT: No, my friend. You do not see it yet, but you are as connected to the ancient, slumbering horrors as I am. You are their servant, and they will lead you to your answers.

FRANK: I'm just an artist! Was, I mean. I ain't….

LYNCROFT: What happened, Mr Ellery? What took a promising illustrator and turned him into…you?

FRANK: None of your goddamn business is what. Where were you the night Bernie was murdered?

LYNCROFT: Here. Alone.

FRANK: That's a piss-poor alibi.

LYNCROFT: Nevertheless, it is the truth. I am often here, and always alone.

FRANK: What about Bernie? I know he got under most people's skin. He get under yours?

LYNCROFT: I had no feelings about Mr Wolcott one way or the other. He handled my literary affairs and made a decent penny off of my success. I never put more thought into it than that.

FRANK: No resentment there? Bernie cashing in while you do the real work?

LYNCROFT: Does the wolf resent the ravens that eat what he kills?

(Beat. FRANK *pulls out a cigarette.*)

FRANK: Mind if I smoke?

LYNCROFT: Actually, I…

(FRANK *lights it and smokes.*)

FRANK: Here's the thing, Mr Lyncroft. The cops… they got nothin'. They can't figure out the whos and the whys and the wherefors 'cause Bernie lived real private-like. The more I look into it, the more I keep hittin' the same wall: Desiree St Claire, Brad Rayburn, Walter Kingston-Smith and you. You four were the only ones in Bernie's life. Now the guy didn't inspire much by way of affection, so I figure that he had somethin' on you. On each and every one of you. How close am I?

(LYNCROFT *smiles.*)

LYNCROFT: Now you're getting somewhere.

(LYNCROFT *takes* FRANK's *cigarette and puts it out.*)

LYNCROFT: This story begins, and will likely end, with books. I have mine, Mr Wolcott had his.

FRANK: The police didn't take any of Bernie's books.

LYNCROFT: Because they didn't know what they were looking for.

FRANK: Which was?

LYNCROFT: A small book, black leather cover, with the initials B.W. inscribed on the cover.

FRANK: Bernard Wolcott.

LYNCROFT: Bravo. You must be a detective.

FRANK: A journal.

LYNCROFT: Yes. If you're looking for Wolcott's secrets, I'd start there. Now go.

(*A strange, alien sound from the other room. The lights flicker again, and something strange and alien moves in the shadows.*)

LYNCROFT: It would appear that my guest has arrived.

(*The strange sound, almost a bestial roar, grows louder.* FRANK *runs. Lights change.*)

Scene 5

FRANK: (*V O*) I couldn't amscray fast enough. There was something about Lyncroft…something wrong. And it spread out to anything around him. Whoever… whatever was behind that door, I didn't want to know. What I did know was I had a lead, my first solid one since this whole wingding started. I had to get to the crime scene, so I played the payola game again. Money exchanged hands, and I was in. Normally, I don't bother with the crime scene this long after the fact. The cops've usually snagged anything worth snagging, and made a pigsty of the rest. But I had a feeling they missed something this time; something I sure as hellfire had to find.

(*The bedroom of Bernard Wolcott. It is in shambles.* FRANK *is stalking around, making notes. He stops, noticing a small handkerchief covered in blood. He lifts it up.*)

FRANK: Well, what do we have…?

(*Suddenly, a voice in the dark—*)

WALTER: You don't belong here.

(FRANK *spins, drawing his gun and shining his flashlight. He doesn't spot anyone.*)

WALTER: You're a small man. You would break the law, not to uphold it, but for your own personal gain.

FRANK: Who's there?

WALTER: Darkness. Shadow. The unseen justice that all criminals fear.

(Suddenly, a cloaked man grabs FRANK's *throat.)*

WALTER: They call me...The Cloak!

(In a quick move, FRANK *grabs* WALTER *and hurls him to the ground.)*

WALTER: AH! Damn!

*(*FRANK *points his gun at* WALTER.*)*

FRANK: Don't move, pal. I...

*(*WALTER *rolls into the darkness.* FRANK *shines his light on him.* WALTER *is wearing a nice black suit, and a hooded cloak obscuring most of his face.)*

FRANK: Hey. Fancypants. I said don't move.

WALTER: You caught me by surprise. It won't happen again.

(Beat. FRANK *stares at* WALTER *for a bit.)*

FRANK: Walter? That you? Walter Kingston-Smith?

(Beat)

WALTER: I am the moonless night that descends upon those who would harm this city...

FRANK: It is you, isn't it?

(Beat)

WALTER: No.

FRANK: Jumpin' Jesus...you crack your head or something?

WALTER: I don't know who you think I am...

FRANK: Walter Kingston-Smith.

WALTER: ...but I assure you, I'm not.

FRANK: So you're just some nut dressing up like a hero-mag character? A character written by Walter Kingston-Smith?

(Beat)

WALTER: I am the reason you fear the dark.

FRANK: Fine. I ain't got time for this bunk.

WALTER: Don't walk away from me. *(He draws a gun.)*

FRANK: Put that away.

WALTER: You're disturbing a crime scene.

FRANK: If you were gonna shoot me, why not do it when I didn't know you were here?

WALTER: Fire-arms are my last resort. I have trained with the yogis of Tibet, the Indian Rajput and the senseis of the Oriental arts.

FRANK: Swell. *(He resumes investigating.)* You want to stop speechifying and help me look?

WALTER: I told you to stop.

FRANK: Yep. And you didn't stop me, so I'm gonna keep looking.

(Beat. WALTER holsters his gun.)

WALTER: Well played.

FRANK: You're the only one playing here. I'm trying to do real detective work.

WALTER: I'm a detective too.

FRANK: Pfft.

WALTER: What was that?

FRANK: What was what?

WALTER: You snorted. Derisively.

FRANK: Never heard someone say that word out loud. You must be a writer.

WALTER: Well, I have been known to… *(Beat)* You think you're pretty clever, don't you?

FRANK: I think I'm God's gift to women. Just can't meet a woman who agrees.

WALTER: What are you here for?

FRANK: You tell me.

WALTER: You want to find Bernard Wolcott's killer.

FRANK: That's what I'm getting paid for.

WALTER: You won't find anything.

FRANK: Somebody said that to Columbus once.

WALTER: I've already done my own investigation. Using methods beyond your understanding.

FRANK: Then why are you here?

(Beat)

WALTER: Just as the night falls on the city, so The Cloak…

FRANK: The little black book. Am I right?

WALTER: The…the what?

FRANK: My guy on the force says they didn't find it when they searched this place. Means it's still around here somewhere. And from what I hear tell, that book has juicy secrets on at least a few of you, maybe all of you. The kind of stuff that would keep a writer who's about to make it big loyal to his bum of an agent.

WALTER: I have no idea what you're talking about.

FRANK: I'll bet you don't.

(FRANK is lifting up a side table.)

WALTER: Found something?

FRANK: Yeah, maybe. Hear that?

(FRANK *shakes it. The sound of a drawer moving in the table.*)

WALTER: What? What am I supposed to be hearing?

FRANK: Sounds like a drawer. 'Cept there ain't no drawer on this table, is there?

WALTER: A secret compartment!

FRANK: That's my thinking.

WALTER: You've done good work…for a reprobate.

FRANK: Thanks?

WALTER: And for the record, I'm sorry.

FRANK: For what?

WALTER: For this.

(WALTER *grabs* FRANK *in a strange headlock.*)

FRANK: Hey!

WALTER: Don't struggle. This is a Bengali Sleep Grip. In a matter of moments, you'll be…

(FRANK *breaks free from* WALTER's *grip.*)

WALTER: Damn!

FRANK: What they hell are you doing?

WALTER: What lies inside that compartment is not for your eyes.

FRANK: Says you! I'm the one who found it.

WALTER: Don't make me…

(FRANK *and* WALTER *draw guns on each other simultaneously.*)

WALTER: Well.

FRANK: Well.

WALTER: Looks like we have a…

(FRANK *fires over* WALTER's *head.* WALTER *lets out a girlish scream and drops his gun.*)

FRANK: Gotta tell ya, Cloak. I read your stories, in the magazines. Never said anything about you screaming like a sissy.

WALTER: Give me my gun back.

(Beat)

FRANK: Yeah, I ain't gonna do that.

WALTER: You don't have to fear me.

FRANK: That's a relief.

WALTER: Why don't you just open the compartment and see what's inside?

FRANK: Why don't you just get lost?

WALTER: I have just as much right to be here as you do.

FRANK: Which is no right at all.

WALTER: Exactly.

(Beat. FRANK *thinks about it.)*

FRANK: Ah, the hell with it. *(He starts trying to open the drawer.)*

WALTER: Do you know why I patrol the city at night, Detective?

FRANK: No. And I don't care.

WALTER: When I was but a child, my parents were travelling in the Caribbean seas. A sudden storm swept over our ship. My parents…didn't survive. I held to the wreckage for dear life, until a group of criminals out of Singapore…

FRANK: Got it.

(FRANK *pops open the drawer.* WALTER *hurries over.* FRANK *opens it, shakes it and hears nothing. He upends the drawer, but nothing falls out.)*

FRANK: Ah hell.

WALTER: Where's the book?

FRANK: Either he didn't hide it here, or someone beat us to it.

WALTER: No!

FRANK: Don't get twitchy. I ain't explored the whole room yet.

WALTER: I have! I went over every inch of this place!

FRANK: And somehow missed the secret drawer in the…

WALTER: Quiet, you! This is a…I mean…I need that book!

FRANK: Why? What's so damn important that Wolcott got hid in there?!

WALTER: As if you don't know!

FRANK: I don't!

(Beat)

WALTER: Really?

(FRANK grabs WALTER.)

FRANK: Listen up, pally. I got the distinct feeling like I'm being jerked around here. Whatever sick little game you and your pals are playing, it ends now.

WALTER: Release me, and I'll tell you what I know.

(FRANK releases him. WALTER goes for his suit pocket.)

FRANK: No funny stuff. You get me?

WALTER: I'm just getting some papers. Something I found before you got here.

(FRANK closes in. When he does, WALTER tosses some powder into his face. FRANK coughs and hacks.)

FRANK: …Jesus Christ…!

WALTER: Don't worry, detective. That's powdered Jumba Root. Your blindness will be temporary. Now if you'll…

(FRANK *fires blindly, startling* WALTER.)

WALTER: The city cries out for her defender. (*He runs out of the room.*)

FRANK: Big mistake, Walter! Big flippin'… (*Beat*) You bolted, didn'tcha? (*No response*) Son of a bitch.

(*Lights change.*)

Scene 6

FRANK: (*V O*) The nutcase was right about one thing; only took a couple of minutes before I could see. Of course, he'd snuck off by then. Two days of investigating, and I hadn't learned much of anything. I knew in my gut that Wolcott's journal was the key to it all. After The Cloak had vanished, I spent three hours tearing old Bernie's place apart, and came up empty. Wherever that book was, it wasn't there. So I staggered back to my office for a belt of scotch, a tin of sardines and hopefully some goddamn perspective. Turns out I never even made it to the sardines.

(*Lights up on the darkened office.* FRANK *staggers through the door, then turns on the light.* DESIREE *is there.*)

DESIREE: Oh, Frank….

FRANK: Holy Moses!

(DESIREE *runs to* FRANK, *embracing him and crying.*)

FRANK: What the hell is this?

DESIREE: It's awful, just awful…

FRANK: Slow down. What are you talkin' about?

DESIREE: Haven't you heard?

FRANK: Heard what?

DESIREE: Poor Bradley's been attacked!

FRANK: What?

DESIREE: I don't know many details. The policeman, when he was able to stop staring at my décolletage, told me that Bradley was accosted in the street. Someone came at him from behind, then clubbed him repeatedly.

FRANK: Jesus Christ.

DESIREE: He's in the hospital now! They say he has a skull fracture!

FRANK: But he's still alive?

DESIREE: Yes, though God only knows if he'll ever regain consciousness! Oh Frank…

(DESIREE *weeps.* FRANK *leads her to the couch. He pulls out the bloody handkerchief he took from Bernie's.)*

FRANK: Hey, hey. Just try to… *(He realizes what he holds and shoves it back in his pocket. He just holds her.)* It's gonna be all right.

DESIREE: How can you say that!? First Bernie, then Bradley…it was that man! I know it was!

FRANK: The fella that's been following you?

DESIREE: Yes. He no doubt killed Bernie, and now he's after the rest of us.

FRANK: You don't know that.

DESIREE: I don't want to die, Frank.

FRANK: Come on. Bradley's still alive. Whoever came after him botched the job.

DESIREE: That's not much comfort.

FRANK: Sorry. I don't have a lot of experience at… comforting.

(DESIREE *grabs* FRANK, *kissing him passionately. He relents at first, then pulls away.*)

FRANK: Whoa. Slow down there.

DESIREE: Don't you find me desirable?

FRANK: Sure, I'm not blind. I mean, I was a few hours ago but…

DESIREE: I'm scared, Frank. And I want to feel something other than fear.

(DESIREE *closes in, but he moves off the couch.*)

FRANK: Doll, you're still a suspect.

DESIREE: I know.

FRANK: I don't hanky-panky with suspects.

DESIREE: Never?

FRANK: No. To be fair, it hasn't really come up before, but… (*He notices some artwork laid across his desk.*) Hey. What the hell is this?

DESIREE: Oh.

FRANK: This is my…I mean…

DESIREE: Please don't be upset with me.

(FRANK *lifts them up, staring at them.*)

DESIREE: I was waiting here for a while, Frank. And I…I'm sorry, but I started snooping. I found those in your closet.

(FRANK *is silent, still staring at them.*)

DESIREE: You drew these, didn't you? This is your artwork?

(FRANK *nods.*)

DESIREE: They're amazing.

FRANK: I ain't looked at these in…years.

DESIREE: Why did you stop?

(FRANK *stares at* DESIREE.)

FRANK: I thought you said you knew who I was.

DESIREE: I knew that you were once an illustrator, then you gave it up. I never knew why.

(FRANK'*s anger rises. He rolls up the pictures.*)

DESIREE: You can tell me, Frank.

FRANK: Why? 'Cause we're so close? Baby, I met you three days ago. Whatever you think there is between us, it ain't there.

DESIREE: We both know that isn't true.

FRANK: You know what your problem is? You're too goddamn used to getting your own way. You smile, bat your eyes, stick your chest out and men just fall over themselves. Well not this man.

DESIREE: Don't say that.

(DESIREE *goes to* FRANK. *He pulls away.*)

FRANK: Get this through your head, lady! I ain't yours to play games with!

DESIREE: I would never…

FRANK: Don't. Don't finish that sentence. You've been toying with me since the start, and I've had it.

DESIREE: I don't know what you mean.

FRANK: How's about the book?

DESIREE: What book?

FRANK: Ha! Nice try. Wolcott's journal. The book that's got all the dirt on you and your buddies!

DESIREE: What are you referring to?

(FRANK *grabs* DESIREE *roughly.*)

FRANK: Stop! Stop lying to me! I don't know what mess you dragged me into, or why you did it, but I'm out. You hear me?

DESIREE: Don't quit the case. I'm begging you.

FRANK: Yeah, any chance to end up on your knees, right?

(DESIREE *slaps* FRANK *hard.*)

DESIREE: I don't know the kind of life you've lived, Mr Ellery, but you will never talk to me that way again.

FRANK: Say it on your way out. I'm done.

(DESIREE *starts to leave, then stops in the doorway.*)

DESIREE: So this is it, then?

FRANK: This is it.

DESIREE: On the job for three days, and you give up already?

FRANK: Don't try to hurt my pride. I got none left.

DESIREE: That's a shame. Because the man who drew those... (*She points to his artwork.*) ...the man who could channel such passion, such sensitivity through his hands and onto paper...that man has much to be proud of. I'd like to meet him one day.

FRANK: He doesn't come around here anymore.

(*Beat*)

DESIREE: Goodbye. (*She turns to go.*)

FRANK: Why do you give two bits what I think?

DESIREE: I'm drawn to you.

FRANK: I'm nothin' special.

(DESIREE *turns around to* FRANK, *smiles.*)

DESIREE: You're the only one in the room who thinks that.

(DESIREE *and* FRANK *stare at each other for a beat. He slowly leans in and kisses her. They become more passionate. She takes his hands, guiding them. He winces.*)

DESIREE: What is it?

FRANK: Nothin', I...

DESIREE: Are you hurt?

FRANK: It's nothing you did. I just...

(FRANK *sits, staring at his hands.* DESIREE *sits with him.*)

FRANK: These used to be my whole life.

DESIREE: When you were an artist?

FRANK: Yeah. It was the only thing that made me somethin', you know? I could always...I'd get this picture in my head, clear as a bell. And anything I could see in my head, I could put down on paper, exactly the way I imagined it. I loved that. Loved being able to do that.

DESIREE: You talk as though your gift was gone.

FRANK: It is.

DESIREE: I don't believe that.

FRANK: Doesn't make it any less true. (*He crosses away, pours himself a drink.*) This was twenty years ago. I was young. Young and stupid. I had this woman...beautiful woman. Her name was April, and she was sweet as the first breeze of Spring. She would pose for me. Most of the women in my pictures, they were her. I loved her, Desiree. That kind of love that...it's in your skin, you know? Like you can feel it in every nerve.

DESIREE: Yes. I know.

FRANK: Thing is, I wasn't the only one who loved her. (*He drinks.*) Ever heard of Enzo Falconi?

DESIREE: The mobster?

FRANK: I sure as hell ain't talking about Enzo Falconi, the dry cleaner.

DESIREE: Point taken.

FRANK: This guy…this big-time criminal…he'd set his sights on April too. God knows why. Son of a bitch had a wife, a daughter, the whole shebang. But I guess that don't matter now. Turns out April had been on Falconi's lap since before she and I met. *(Beat)* Thing is, Falconi's a reader. One day, he's flipping through Dime Mystery, and who does he see on the cover, hangin' over a vat of acid?

DESIREE: April.

FRANK: Bullseye. So he has his boys buy up more of the mags I drew for. There she is again, lyin' in the back of a town car, swingin' through vines in the jungle. Enzo blows a fuse, has his boys pay me a visit. *(He pours himself another drink.)* When I come to, first thing I see is April cryin' her baby-blues out. Ezno's screamin' at her. Son of a bitch grabs a Remington and points it at my head. I think my number's up, but… He didn't shoot. But I'll tell ya, sometimes I wish he had. *(He drinks.)* He has one of his boys hold me down. Then Enzo… *(Beat)* …he grabs my hand. Holds it against a table so I can see it. And then he…he took the butt of the gun and…

(Beat. DESIREE goes to FRANK.)

FRANK: When he was done, both my hands were bloody pulps. The doctor said I'd never be able to write again, much less draw. And now…they're all but useless. I can write, but they shake real bad when I use a pencil. And they hurt.

DESIREE: Even now?

FRANK: Yeah. *(He holds his hands up.)* They may look all right on the outside, but inside they're broken. Just like me.

(DESIREE takes FRANK's hands.)

FRANK: Don't.

DESIREE: It's all right.

FRANK: Please, I...

(DESIREE kisses them.)

DESIREE: Do they still hurt?

FRANK: Yeah.

(DESIREE kisses FRANK's palm.)

DESIREE: How about now?

FRANK: ...a little...

(DESIREE places them on her waist, and leans in close.)

DESIREE: You don't seem broken to me.

(DESIREE kisses FRANK gently. He grabs her and they fall onto the couch. Lights fade.)

Scene 7

(During the voiceover, FRANK rises from the couch without waking DESIREE.)

FRANK: *(V O)* Desiree St Clair writes romance stories. Hot, steamy, bang-the-headboard romance stories. And after that night, I knew that she was writin' from experience. For the first time in a long time, I used my hands the way God intended. There's this thing, see, when the past disappears. There's just the here and the now, and all that matters is the moment you're in. Desiree gave me that. But when I opened my

eyes again, it was all still there. The case, and all my
questions.

(FRANK *crosses to his desk, grabs his cigarette pack.*)

FRANK: *(V O)* Bernie Wolcott asked me somethin', long
time ago. He wanted to know how an artist ends up as
a P I.

(FRANK *checks the pack. It's empty.*)

FRANK: Damn.

FRANK: *(V O)* I said to him, I said, "Bernie, know what
made me such a good illustrator? 'Cause it's the same
thing that makes me a good P I." And Bernie just shook
his head.

(FRANK *looks to* DESIREE, *makes sure she's still asleep.*)

FRANK: *(V O)* "Details, pally. I'm real, real good with
the details."

(FRANK *goes to* DESIREE's *purse, opens it and begins to
rummage inside. He pulls out a pack of cigarettes.*)

FRANK: *(V O)* See, the best stories out there…they're
all about the details. Those little things that seem
inconsequential…

(FRANK *lights one up, then checks to make sure* DESIREE *is
asleep again. He then goes through her purse.*)

FRANK: *(V O)* …those are the things you gotta keep an
eye on. Read enough pulps, you learn that nothing's
accidental. Sure, I may not be able to draw anymore,
but I'm still in love with the details. 'Cause you never
know. Something simple might be what blows the case
wide open.

(FRANK *pulls a small black book out of* DESIREE's *purse.*)

FRANK: I'll be damned.

(*As* FRANK *opens it, we see the initials "B. W." on the
cover.*)

(Lights fade.)

END OF ACT ONE

ACT TWO

Scene 1

(Darkness. Not long after the last scene)

FRANK: *(V O)* Reality…it's the thing we all gotta live with. From the first time we fall as a baby til the day we die, we're just trying to put it all together. As an adult, you get full of it, think you got it all figured out. Don't feel bad, we all do it. Too damn scary to think otherwise. But this case…The Bernie Wolcott Case… by the end of it, I couldn't ignore the truth anymore. Reality is a con, a suckers game we buy into every single day. But not me. Not after what I seen. And just what did I see? Just you wait. And see.

(DESIREE has gotten up during the voice- over. FRANK lights his cigarette. She is startled by the light.)

DESIREE: Oh!

FRANK: I'd say "good morning", but that moon would make me a liar.

DESIREE: I imagine it will be morning soon enough.

FRANK: Yep. 'Cept I'll probably be a liar in the daylight too.

(Beat)

DESIREE: I'm not sure I follow.

FRANK: Really? I figured you bein' the expert on lying, you'd have some…whaddya call it…insight.

DESIREE: I know it's been a while since you've been with a woman, Frank, but this is hardly a sterling example of post-coital conversation.

FRANK: You feel that string in front of ya? Give it a tug. About time we put some light on things.

(DESIREE *turns on the lights.* FRANK *is sitting, holding the black book.*)

FRANK: I did some reading tonight. Lit by a match so as not to wake ya.

DESIREE: All right.

FRANK: Recognize this? (*He holds the book up.*)

DESIREE: I imagine it's the book you were talking about earlier.

FRANK: You bet your sweet fanny it is.

DESIREE: Charming.

FRANK: And you'll never guess where I found it. In your purse.

DESIREE: What?

FRANK: Since you took my smokes last time, I figured I'd return the favor. Imagine my surprise when I found this tucked away in there.

DESIREE: You went through my purse?

FRANK: Jesus, Bianca. That's what you're worried about?

(*Beat*)

DESIREE: What did you call me?

FRANK: Bianca. That is your name, ain't it? Bianca Fiore Falconi?

(DESIREE *is silent.*)

FRANK: This book here…Real page turner. It was written by our old pal Bernie Wolcott. Most of it, anyway. Got some pages tucked in the back written in some crazy scribble I don't recognize. But the stuff Bernie wrote? Interesting tidbits on Bradley, on Walter…and on you. For example, I didn't know that you were Italian. Name like "Desiree St Clair", why would I? Thing is, Desiree is just one of them… whaddya call it…pseudonyms.

DESIREE: Let me explain…

FRANK: Another interesting detail here… One Miss Bianca Falconi is in fact the daughter of Enzo Falconi! You remember, the man responsible for destroying my life!

DESIREE: Frank, please!

(FRANK *rises, crosses to* DESIREE.)

FRANK: Why? That's all I wanna know? Why me?

DESIREE: I know it might sound strange, but…

FRANK: Strange?! The last three days, I seen all sorts of strange. What I never once, in all my life, expected to see was me lyin' next to the daughter of the man I hate most in this world!

DESIREE: Please listen…

FRANK: So here I am, Desiree Bianca Falconi St Clair, like one of your faithful readers. Amaze me! I'm just dyin' to know what the big twist is gonna be!

DESIREE: Frank…

FRANK: Why the hell are you here?!

DESIREE: Because I love you! *(Beat)* I have loved you since I was sixteen years old.

FRANK: Peddle your malarkey somewhere else. I ain't buyin'.

DESIREE: Scoff all you want, but it's true.

FRANK: What do you know from the truth?

DESIREE: They don't call it "true love" for nothing.

(FRANK *walks away, pours himself a drink.*)

DESIREE: One day, when I was still just a girl, I was in my father's study. I had a deep love for the written word, even then. Daddy had a large pile of magazines…pulp trades. I was going to push them aside; I was looking for my Voltaire. But then I looked down, and the picture of a woman looked up at me. A drawing, actually, of the most beautiful woman I'd ever seen. She was facing off against some strange, tentacled thing oozing out of a crater. The other people around her were running, but she was holding her ground. It wasn't her figure or her face that made her beautiful, no. It was her strength. Defiant and fierce and…stunning. I'd never seen anything like it, and then I grabbed another magazine, and there she was again, and again, and again. On each cover, she was a different character, in different clothes, in different places, but they were all her. And Frank…I could feel your love for her. So much passion in every stroke of your brush. I never knew a man could feel that way about a woman. My father was…cold. Distant. Nothing like the artist behind those covers. I didn't learn why my father had those magazines until later. *(Beat)* Not long after my father attacked you, things went very badly for him. He made the wrong enemies.

FRANK: Look how I weep.

DESIREE: To protect us, he sent my mother and me away. A new place, with new names. Bianca Falconi became Desiree St Clair. But before I left, I…I knew I had to meet you. I wanted to see Francis Ellery with my own eyes. By the time I worked up the courage to seek you out, you were in the hospital. I visited you once, only once, while you were still there.

FRANK: Like hell.

DESIREE: It's the truth. You were sleeping. I imagine they gave you something very strong when they...reset the bones in your hands. I wish you could have seen the surprise on my face. I had imagined Francis Ellery to be an old man, with pinched eyes and no hair to speak of...but here was this handsome young man.

FRANK: You spin a pretty yarn, sister, but it all sounds like bunk to me.

DESIREE: "Fill your paper with the breathings of your heart."

(Beat)

FRANK: What did you say?

DESIREE: I left you a present on your nightstand. A sterling silver pen, with an inscription. "Fill your paper with the breathings of your heart."

FRANK: That don't mean anything to me.

DESIREE: When we first met, I took a pen from your desk. That pen. I saw it with my own eyes.

(Beat)

FRANK: Why didn't you tell me this before?

DESIREE: Would you have let me walk through that door if you knew who I was, who I really was?

FRANK: Let's say I believe a word of this hooey...

DESIREE: Everything I said, I...

FRANK: Let's say I believe it. How the hell am I supposed to believe anything you say, from this point forward? You lied to me about this book without batting an eye.

DESIREE: I swear to you, I have no idea why that book was in my purse.

FRANK: Can ya maybe see why I'm having a hard time buying that?

DESIREE: I can't imagine that it paints me in a flattering light. Would I have hired you for this case if…?

FRANK: Christ, what about the case? Lemme paint you a picture: The main reason the cops ain't dragged you and your buddies in is because they can't find no motive. Then they get hold of this book. It's got all these great little secrets about Bernie's last clients, the kind that he was probably using to blackmail the lot of ya.

DESIREE: There may be some truth to that, but…

FRANK: I bet plenty of Enzo's old colleagues would love to get their hands on his daughter, 'cept they can't find her. I bet Bernie figured that out too. Why else would a writer like you stick with a hack agent like him? Huh?

DESIREE: That's just conjecture!

FRANK: It's enough for any halfwit prosecutor to make a hell of a case. And for the record, your honor, sleeping with the detective *you* hired sure as hell don't help!

DESIREE: Do you want me to say I made mistakes? Yes! I made mistakes! But I don't regret my actions, Frank. *(She goes to him.)* Last night, you felt something. I know it. For a brief moment, the man you once were lived again. That man loved me as deeply and as truly as I love him.

FRANK: This ain't one of your stories.

DESIREE: You're right. Real life is so much more…vivid.

(DESIREE kisses FRANK. He gives in to it, then breaks away.)

DESIREE: Frank…

FRANK: Goddammit! I can't see straight with you…just get out!

DESIREE: You don't want that.

FRANK: Don't talk like you know my mind!

(FRANK *drags* DESIREE *to the door.*)

DESIREE: This isn't you. This isn't who you were meant to be.

FRANK: You know what your problem is, doll? You invested so much in who you thought I was, there ain't no way I could live up to it. The drunken, pissed-off wreck you see before ya? THIS is Frank Ellery. Always has been. Always been a has-been.

(FRANK *opens the door.* DESIREE *stares at him for a bit, deeply hurt.*)

DESIREE: Well, I suppose it wouldn't be a romance without a broken heart or two.

(DESIREE *exits. Lights change.*)

Scene 2

FRANK: *(V O)* After our spat, I showered off what I could and headed to the hospital. I wanted to see our boy Brad. Who knows why? I wasn't even sure I was on the case anymore, but…well, it was just like Desiree…Bianca…just like she said. Poor bastard had his damn skull caved in. He was alive, but sleeping deeper than Snow White. The nurse said they didn't know if he'd ever wake up. She also said I wasn't his only visitor. Not ten minutes before I got there, another fella had come and went. Thin man in a black suit, smelled like a fresh-dug grave. Said he had paint on his hands. Didn't take me a second to figure out who it was. I asked the nurse where he went. And when she answered, I right away wished she hadn't.

(*Lights rise on an asylum ward in the hospital. It is grim and eerie, with a flickering light illuminating the dank room.*

The sounds of screams can be heard offstage. LYNCROFT *is alone, writing.* FRANK *enters.)*

FRANK: Didn't know the hospital had a loony bin.

LYNCROFT: Asylum, actually. And yes, it does.

*(*LYNCROFT *turns to see* FRANK.*)*

LYNCROFT: How are you, Mr Ellery?

FRANK: Better than our mutual pal.

LYNCROFT: Yes. I was visiting him earlier. I meant to go straight home, but…this place called to me.

FRANK: Swell.

LYNCROFT: Is that why you were here? To see after Bradley? *(He nods.)*

FRANK: Surprised to see you here.

LYNCROFT: Yes?

FRANK: You don't strike me as real sentimental.

LYNCROFT: I'm not a monster, Mr Ellery. Bradley was a gentle fellow, and didn't deserve this.

(A violent scream. LYNCROFT *breathes deeply, enrapt.)*

LYNCROFT: This is a place of glorious sounds. Listen to them all.

FRANK: Hard not to.

LYNCROFT: It's a beautiful song, for those who know the words.

FRANK: You one of 'em?

LYNCROFT: I am. I spent several years in this very asylum.

FRANK: That a fact?

LYNCROFT: Oh yes. My mother was quite mad, you see. Murdered my father in cold blood. I witnessed it all. I was ten at the time, and ill-prepared to process what had happened. These walls raised me during my tender years. It is one of the few places that still feels like…home. *(Beat)* Madness isn't so terrible a thing, Mr Ellery. It's simply an altered perception, an awareness of something outside the world we know. There are those who flee from that perception. Others embrace it.

FRANK: Sounds like you need one of them funny jackets.

LYNCROFT: Never dismiss a man because of insanity. In many ways, he's freer than you will ever be.

FRANK: Freer than you or I, you mean.

LYNCROFT: Do I?

(Beat. FRANK chuckles.)

FRANK: I'll tell ya, I thought this whole morbid shtick was an act; a face you put on in public. But it ain't, is it? You really are a fruitcake.

LYNCROFT: If it makes you more comfortable to think of me that way, then by all means. *(Beat)* I know this may be hard to believe, but I am trying to help you.

FRANK: What I don't get is why. You've been slammed by critics, and you don't care. You stroll around in a nuthouse, and you don't care. So why do you care about this?

LYNCROFT: Desiree, Bradley, Walter…even you. We're all artists, connected in a way that…means something. I don't know how to explain it better than that.

(Beat)

FRANK: I got the book.

LYNCROFT: One of mine? Do you wish an autograph?

FRANK: The black book. Bernie's black book.

LYNCROFT: Ah. Well done. Did it illuminate your search?

FRANK: Answered some questions, made me ask a lot more.

LYNCROFT: That is the way of information.

FRANK: My biggest question is…why don't it have any dirt on you?

(LYNCROFT *stares at* FRANK. FRANK *takes the book out of his pocket, flips through it.*)

FRANK: It's a tawdry little thing filled with all sorts of trash about your friends Desiree and Walter and Bradley. But not a peep about you.

LYNCROFT: I don't have an answer for that.

FRANK: Why don't I believe you?

LYNCROFT: I'm the one who led you to the book. Would I do so if it would implicate me?

(FRANK *takes a paper that had been tucked into the book and hands it to* LYNCROFT.)

FRANK: How's about this?

LYNCROFT: What is it?

FRANK: Something I found tucked between the pages.

LYNCROFT: It's old. Very old.

FRANK: Yeah. And I can't make heads or tails out of that language. If it is a language.

LYNCROFT: Why bring it to me?

FRANK: You're always writing about old books full of evil stuff. Figured it might belong to you.

LYNCROFT: What I write is fiction, Mr Ellery.

FRANK: See, I think that, but I'm not convinced that you do.

(FRANK *takes the page back from* LYNCROFT, *then puts the book and page back in his coat pocket. As they speak,* LYNCROFT *puts on a pair of gloves, preparing to leave.*)

LYNCROFT: It would be easy to make me the villain here, Mr Ellery, but it doesn't make it true.

FRANK: Why do I get the feelin' like there's a bigger picture here, and you and your pals are workin' real hard to keep me from seein' it?

LYNCROFT: They are not my friends, sir. I have no friends. But if you're feeling a bit…phobic, perhaps I could arrange a room for you here.

(FRANK *grabs* LYNCROFT *roughly.*)

FRANK: I should thank you, freakshow. I was one step away from throwin' this whole case behind me, but now… Lemme make this real clear. I'm coming for you. I'm coming for all of you. Whoever killed Bernie Wolcott is going down hard. You get me?

LYNCROFT: Oh yes. I get you.

(*The lights flicker, then sputter out. The screams intensify. When the light returns,* FRANK *is kneeling on the ground,* LYNCROFT *behind him with a hand on* FRANK's *mouth.*)

LYNCROFT: My father was a scholar, a student of the ancient world. He had taken us to the subcontinent when I was only a boy. He found an ancient book there that spoke of the final days, a book that became his obsession. When we returned, my mother took a hatchet to him. Except that it wasn't my mother anymore, Mr Ellery. It was a creature of a bygone age, wearing her form. That was why I had to kill her. The court called it self-defense, and locked me in this dungeon. I told you before, this is my home and I am the lord over all who dwell here. Even you.

(FRANK *struggles, but* LYNCROFT *holds him fast. The shadows move around them.*)

FRANK: This ain't one of your stories, Lyncroft!

LYNCROFT: I'll be the judge of that.

(LYNCROFT *releases* FRANK *and the room fills with strobing lights. The screams grow louder. When the strobe effect is over, lights return to normal and* LYNCROFT *is gone.*)

FRANK: Jesus Christ.

(*Lights fade.*)

Scene 3

FRANK: (*V O*) And so I went back to my office. Truth is, I ran there. Don't get me wrong; it's hard to rattle my cage, but everything about Lyncroft was designed for rattling. The fact that Bernie didn't have any dirt on him…it shoulda made Lyncroft seem more innocent. I don't know why, but it just made me more worried about him. So yeah, back in the office. I lit me up the last of Desiree's cigarettes and started going through the black book. I felt kind funny in my head, so I closed my eyes for a second. I did not like what I saw when I opened 'em.

(FRANK *awakens in his chair, staring at at* WALTER *dressed as the Cloak.*)

FRANK: Ah, for Christ's sake. What're you…? (*He gets up, then immediately starts to wobble.*) Oh…oh god…

WALTER: Feeling poorly?

FRANK: …what'd you…do to me…?

WALTER: This.

(WALTER *grabs him and empties a vial into his mouth. He closes* FRANK'S *mouth.* FRANK *struggles, then swallows it.*)

FRANK: What the hell was that?

WALTER: Anti-toxin.

FRANK: What the what?

WALTER: An antidote.

FRANK: I was poisoned?

WALTER: Yes.

FRANK: The hell you say. I…I…uh-oh…

(FRANK *rushes to the bathroom and vomits.*)

WALTER: Don't fight it, Mr Ellery. Your body is purging itself of a very rare and deadly venom.

FRANK: Wonderful. *(He vomits again.)*

WALTER: It may take a while.

FRANK: I hate you. *(He vomits again.)*

WALTER: I got here perhaps half an hour ago. You were barely breathing, and your lips had turned blue. What do you remember?

(FRANK *walks out of the bathroom.*)

FRANK: I was visiting Rayburn at the hospital. I got back and…actually, I was feeling kinda funny before I fell asleep.

WALTER: Based on your symptoms and the odd citric scent on your mouth, I believe you were dosed with aconite.

FRANK: Wait. How close were you to my mouth?

WALTER: Also known as The Queen of Poisons or Devil's Helmet, it is an Asian flower of extreme toxicity. Had I not administered the remedy when I did, you would most likely be dead now.

FRANK: What the hell are you talking about?

WALTER: Isn't it obvious? Someone tried to kill you. Have you ingested anything strange in the last few hours?

FRANK: No. I've been runnin' on cheap scotch and cigarettes for… *(Beat. He goes to the ashtray.)* Desiree.

WALTER: St Clair?

FRANK: No, the Queen of Sweden. She left her cigarettes here. I smoked one right before I passed out.

WALTER: What was the Queen of Sweden doing here?

FRANK: Desiree St Clair, you moron!

WALTER: Oh. That makes more sense.

FRANK: We got in a fight.

WALTER: Hardly a reason to poison someone.

FRANK: I think she knows I'm close.

(WALTER *removes the cigarette butt.*)

WALTER: …not much here. I'll have to examine it at my lab…

FRANK: This proves it. I got the answers now. I just gotta put 'em in the right order.

WALTER: You know who killed Mr Wolcott?

FRANK: Not yet, but soon. It's all in the little black book. *(Beat)* Where's the book?

WALTER: Bernie's book? You have Bernie's book?

FRANK: It was right there when I went to sleep.

WALTER: Dammit! She must have crept in after the aconite had taken effect and stolen the book! She could be anywhere by now! Damn you, Desiree St Clair! You win this round, but don't get comfortable. The Cloak doesn't call off the hunt that easily!

(Beat)

FRANK: Gimme the book, Walter.

WALTER: I don't have the book. And I'm not Walter!

FRANK: I know you think you're protecting yourself, but I already read it. Hiding it is just gonna make it harder for me to put this all together.

WALTER: Then…then you know my dread secret.

FRANK: Yep.

WALTER: You know that The Cloak is in all reality…
(He removes his cloak.) …Walter Kingston-Smith.

(Beat)

FRANK: But how?

WALTER: That question has kept the police of this city
up at night. By day, I'm a wealthy man about town.
But when the sun sets, I prowl the streets providing
justice for those who need it most.

FRANK: And Bernie was using this to queer the deal
with C B S, wasn't he?

WALTER: Yes. Somehow he was able to see through my
disguise.

FRANK: Mm-hmm.

WALTER: He threatened to expose my double-life if I
didn't cut him in on the radio-show profits. Seventy-
five percent for him, thirty-five percent for me.

FRANK: That's some deal.

WALTER: Yes. The fiend had me by the shorthairs and
he knew it! *(Beat)* But that doesn't mean I killed him.

FRANK: Here's what I'm wondering. What if you came
in here, gave me some ipecac and tried to get me to
think I was poisoned? You know, to point the blame at
someone else.

WALTER: I would never do that.

FRANK: Most people wouldn't run around in a cape,
but here you are.

WALTER: Believe what you want to, detective. I'm the
one who saved your life.

FRANK: Yeah? Why?

WALTER: I hated Bernard Wolcott, I admit. But I hate crime even more. Whatever sins he committed, they were for a court to decide, not some common murderer. *(Beat)* I've been following you, Mr Ellery, because I believe I cannot solve this case on my own. Do you think you can?

FRANK: I'm getting there.

WALTER: The longer you take, the colder the trail goes. If we work together…

FRANK: Nope.

WALTER: …we can…will you let me finish?

FRANK: I don't have partners.

WALTER: Let me put it this way. I have access to a great deal of wealth. And a pretty keen crime lab. You have… *(He gestures to the office.)*

FRANK: It's a lot nicer when it's clean.

WALTER: I'm certain. *(He tosses him the book.)* You're onto something with this. Keep it. Learn what you can from it.

FRANK: What're you gonna do?

WALTER: I have informants. I'm going to keep tabs on the other suspects. *(He offers his hand.)*

FRANK: I still think you coulda done it.

WALTER: I'm going to prove you wrong.

(FRANK shakes WALTER's hand.)

WALTER: And here I thought you might spit in it. *(He dons his cloak and runs to the window. He throws it open.)*

FRANK: What are you doing? The door is right…

WALTER: The night calls to me! *(He jumps out the window.)*

FRANK: …there. *(Beat)* Moron.

(Lights change.)

Scene 4

FRANK: *(V O)* So there it was, for better or worse. I had a partner. Sure he was an idiot, but even a broken clock is right twice a day. I had to get this thing solved and fast. Someone had already taken a pipe to Bradley's head, and I had a feeling that was just the beginning. I had the book, I had some details…it felt like I had all the pieces in front of me and I just needed to see how they all fit. The cops had nothing on Bradley's attacker. The bum hit him at night, in an alley. No fingerprints, no witnesses, no suspects. So I decided to check out the poor guy's apartment, take a look-see.

(Lights up on BRADLEY's *flat.* FRANK *is going through things. He ends up with* BRADLEY's *breathing apparatus. He stares at it, chuckles, perhaps even tries it on. Suddenly, a gout of colored smoke appears in a corner.* FRANK *backs away, drawing his pistol.)*

FRANK: The hell is this?

(Coughing from inside the cloud. BRADLEY *steps out of it. He is now an old man in his eighties, with a strange device around his chest. He has a briefcase.)*

BRADLEY: Oh god…what a stink…

*(*BRADLEY *removes an asthma inhaler, uses it.)*

FRANK: Who the hell are you?

BRADLEY: Damned temporal discharge…always leaves a cloud of this stuff…sorry…just give me a… *(He uses the inhaler again.)* Ahhh….there we go.

FRANK: Listen up, Pops. I don't know who you are, but…

BRADLEY: Frank!

(Beat)

FRANK: But I guess you know who I am.

(BRADLEY *shuffles around, examining. He goes to* FRANK.)

FRANK: Whoa. Slow down there.

(BRADLEY *places his hands on* FRANK's *face.*)

BRADLEY: My god…just like I remember. *(He sees his old breathing apparatus.)* HA! Would you look at that! Why, I haven't seen this old beauty in sixty years!

FRANK: Just tell me who the hell you are!

BRADLEY: Ah! Of course. Sorry, I wander and… *(He straightens up.)* I am Bradley Rayburn, and I come… FROM THE FUTURE!

FRANK: You gotta be kiddin' me.

BRADLEY: It's true. Dramatic presentation aside, it's me, Frank! It's Brad!

FRANK: I saw Brad yesterday. He's a kid of twenty-two with a caved-in coconut.

BRADLEY: So…that makes this…one moment… *(He checks the gauges on his device.)* 1933, right?

FRANK: What?

BRADLEY: What day is it!?

FRANK: March 9th.

BRADLEY: Holy Moses! It worked! The damn thing actually worked! HA!

(BRADLEY *grabs* FRANK, *kisses him.*)

FRANK: Stop that!

BRADLEY: So if this is…wait, you're here.

FRANK: I…am?

BRADLEY: That means you're already investigating the murder!

FRANK: What the hell else would I…?

BRADLEY: NO! NO NO NO! DAMMIT! *(He starts fidgeting with the device, furious.)* This infernal contraption! I was trying to go back before Bernie was killed! I was so close! SO DAMN CLOSE! *(He collapses into a chair.)* You have no idea! Ten years! Ten years I spent working on this thing! The trick was finding something that could alter the physics; that was the trick, yes. Then I got my hands on this…

(FRANK grabs BRADLEY.)

FRANK: You are not Bradley Rayburn.

BRADLEY: Oh, Francis. Don't let the white hair and whiskers fool you. I always assumed you were smarter than that. Of course, we didn't know each other long, but…

FRANK: So…what? You built some sort of…?

BRADLEY: You don't want to say "time machine", do you?

FRANK: No. I don't.

BRADLEY: But I did! I did it, Frank! All my years of tinkering with technology, and…this was the key! *(He removes a stone from his device.)* This little beauty here. It's a fragment of a meteor that fell from the heavens in 1982. It contained an element unlike any we'd ever seen. I call it Rayburnium.

FRANK: Come on.

BRADLEY: What it does, you see…this allows me to fold time…connecting a point in my present to a point in my past. Einstein had a theory that…You have no idea who Einstein is, do you?

FRANK: He sure as hell ain't my sister.

BRADLEY: All that matters is that I'm here. Now.

FRANK: Prove it.

BRADLEY: I thought I just did.

FRANK: Prove that you're Brad Rayburn.

BRADLEY: Oh. I…um…hmm…OH! I know! Do you have the book?

FRANK: What book?

BRADLEY: The little black book. You know the one.

FRANK: How do you know about it?

(Beat)

BRADLEY: Because I was the one who put it in Desiree's purse.

FRANK: How's that?

BRADLEY: I…god, I still remember it like it was yesterday…when I found Bernie dead that night, I panicked. I thought someone had gotten hold of his book and…I found it. But when you came along, started asking all your questions, I…do you remember the night of Lyncroft's reading?

FRANK: Sure.

BRADLEY: When I went to get Desiree's coat and purse. That's when I did it. I was afraid that, if you found out I had it, that you'd assume I killed Bernie.

FRANK: Because you and he were lovers.

(Beat)

BRADLEY: You've read it then.

FRANK: Cover to cover. Right before I tossed Desiree out on her ear for hiding it from me.

BRADLEY: Ah. Yes. I…yes, I should apologize about that.

FRANK: Jesus Christ…it really is you, isn't it?

BRADLEY: In the saggy, liver-spotted flesh.

FRANK: Just when I thought this couldn't get more nuts, here comes space man from the glorious future.

BRADLEY: I wish, Frank. God, how I wish. *(He sits.)* The future is awful. Nothing like how I thought it would be. No flying cars. No visitors from another planet. Just....people living with no sense of wonder, no hope for what is coming next. Oh, it used to be there. The Fifties, the Sixties...god, the Sixties...we went to the moon, Frank!

FRANK: Come on.

BRADLEY: It's true! We walked on its surface! But those days are gone. Now people just walk around bitching about the here and now. They look at the future and see nothing but more bleak hopelessness. We used to be a people of exploration, of imagination. Now we're just...boring and miserable and....

FRANK: Is this a speech?

BRADLEY: Some of it. I was the graduation speaker at Harvard last year. I...don't think they'll be having me back.

FRANK: So why the hell did you come back to this?

BRADLEY: You've read the book, Frank. You know why.

FRANK: 'Cause of Bernie?

BRADLEY: I loved him. And he loved me. I was trying to go back before he was murdered. It's hard to get an accurate reading on this damn thing.

FRANK: So go back further.

BRADLEY: I can't. There's only enough Rayburnium for one trip to the past, then back.

(FRANK sits.)

FRANK: Jesus, I need a drink.

BRADLEY: Time travel gets tricky. That's why I never wrote about it. Too much damn explaining and…

FRANK: I gotta ask. Did I end up solving this thing?

(Beat)

BRADLEY: No.

FRANK: Goddammit. What happened?

BRADLEY: I don't…I'm not sure.

FRANK: Why? Didn't you ask me when you woke up?

BRADLEY: You have to understand. I was in that coma for two years. When I came out of it, you were…

(Beat)

FRANK: I was what?

BRADLEY: Probably best if I don't say.

FRANK: Dead?

BRADLEY: Well…

FRANK: Jesus Christ! I'm gonna be dead in two years?!

BRADLEY: I don't know.

FRANK: Look, don't spare my feelings, pal. If I took a dirt-nap, at least…

BRADLEY: No one knows what happened to you, Frank.

FRANK: Come again?

BRADLEY: You, Desiree, Walter, Lyncroft. Nobody knows.

FRANK: How is that even possible? *(Beat)* Is this like them stories, where you can't talk about the future 'cause you don't want to change it or…?

BRADLEY: Oh, balls to that! Of course I want to change the future! It's the worst!

FRANK: So what happened?

BRADLEY: An earthquake. A big one. Took out a good chunk of Los Angeles.

FRANK: When?

BRADLEY: I…dammit, when was it…?

FRANK: You don't remember?!

BRADLEY: Hey! I had a skull fracture! And I'm ninety years old! You're lucky I've still got any marbles at all!

FRANK: Fair enough.

BRADLEY: I tried, Frank. I came back, tried to learn what happened but…a lot of people died in that earthquake. And a lot of bodies were just…never found.

FRANK: Like mine.

BRADLEY: After all that had happened, all that destruction, solving the murder of a washed-up agent wasn't high on anyone's list anymore.

FRANK: Except yours.

(Beat)

BRADLEY: I still see him, sometimes. I dream about it. We'd had a fight. I left to cool off at a jazz club and… when I came back, there he was. His chest ripped apart and…I'm not going to tell you he was a good man, Frank. But he was mine. The world would be an easier place if we got to pick who we loved.

FRANK: You got that right.

BRADLEY: That's why I spent so long trying to figure out time travel. I thought I could go back and save him but…Bradley Rayburn drops the ball again.

FRANK: Gotta tell ya, that's a hell of a ways to go for love.

BRADLEY: It's not so crazy. That kind of passion…that kind of loss…it stays with you, no matter how hard you try to let it go. First loves are usually the deepest.

FRANK: Jeez. You shoulda been writin' romances.

BRADLEY: That was Desiree's genre. And she knew far better than I ever did.

(FRANK *rises.*)

BRADLEY: Something I said?

(FRANK *lights a cigarette.*)

BRADLEY: You love her, don't you?

FRANK: Hell if I know.

BRADLEY: You know. You just wish you didn't.

FRANK: I mean…she made me feel something. Something like being alive again. But….

BRADLEY: Is it the stuff Bernie wrote in that book? That she's a mobster's daughter?

FRANK: That's…not a small part of it.

BRADLEY: Frank, what a person is doesn't matter. Only what they do. (*Beat. Suddenly he jumps up.*)

BRADLEY: OH! Dammit!

FRANK: What?

BRADLEY: That's what…hold on! (*He opens his briefcase.*)

FRANK: What you got there?

BRADLEY: It's everything I've been able to collect about Bernie's murder over the years.

FRANK: Not much there.

BRADLEY: Earthquakes will do that. Remember this? (*He holds up a much older version of Bernie's black book.*)

FRANK: I'll be damned.

(BRADLEY *gives the briefcase to* FRANK.)

BRADLEY: Any of this look familiar? Or helpful? Anything?

FRANK: Jesus, this stuff looks like it's been through the wringer and back.

BRADLEY: Well, it's sixty-some-odd years old now.

FRANK: Why do you have all this?

BRADLEY: I was trying to figure out what happened to see if I could prevent it but…

(FRANK *holds up a piece of notebook paper.*)

BRADLEY: Find something?

FRANK: This is my handwriting.

BRADLEY: I thought so! I never could read your chicken-scratch!

FRANK: But I didn't write this.

BRADLEY: Probably means you just haven't written it yet. What does it say?

FRANK: "Brown, not red."

(Beat)

BRADLEY: Brown not red?

FRANK: Yep.

BRADLEY: Red the color? Not like you were saying not to read Judith Brown or…?

FRANK: The color.

BRADLEY: Hmm. What do you think it means?

FRANK: I don't know. I haven't written it yet. But it's here. But I haven't written yet. But I…

BRADLEY: Don't think too hard about it, sweetie. You'll get a nosebleed.

(Suddenly, WALTER runs in as The Cloak.)

WALTER: There you are! I've been looking… Who is this?

BRADLEY: Walter?!

WALTER: I am the shadowed hunter…

BRADLEY: Walter! It is you!

(BRADLEY *grabs* WALTER *and kisses him.*)

WALTER: …I…what?

BRADLEY: It's me, Walter! It's Bradley!

WALTER: …I…what?

FRANK: He's traveled back in time to…help us solve the murder, I guess?

(*Beat*)

WALTER: I'm very confused.

BRADLEY: It's true, Walt! Thanks to my discovery of Rayburnium, I…

FRANK: Just go with me on this.

(*Beat*)

WALTER: I don't understand anything that is happening right now!

FRANK: Just…what do you want, Walter?

WALTER: I am not Walter Kingston-Smith. I am…

FRANK: We all know it's you! Just move on!

WALTER: I was attacked, not an hour ago!

FRANK: What?

BRADLEY: You poor boy!

WALTER: I was staking out Bernard's place, waiting to see if the culprit would return to the scene of the crime. Suddenly, I sense someone approaching from behind me, in the shadows. Only my catlike reflexes saved me as he tried to brain me with a pipe.

BRADLEY: Wait…that was exactly what happened to me!

WALTER: Exactly!

FRANK: You sure it was a "he"?

WALTER: I…no, not entirely. He…or she…wore a long coat, and covered her…his face.

BRADLEY: So what happened?

WALTER: I tried to fight him off, but he pulled a knife. We scuffled, and he managed to slice my hand and run.

BRADLEY: Why did he run?

WALTER: Hmm?

BRADLEY: It sounds like he had you on the ropes.

WALTER: It's not important. I…

FRANK: You screamed like a baby, didn't you?

WALTER: IT'S NOT IMPORTANT! The point is, this mysterious attacker is on the move again. What do you think we should do?

BRADLEY: We have to get the others!

FRANK: Slow down. One of you is probably the attacker.

BRADLEY: That's just ridiculous!

FRANK: Ridiculous? RIDICULOUS?! I got Father Time here covered in crazy doodads, I got fancypants doing the world's worst impression of a detective, and I got a whole new definition of "ridiculous."

BRADLEY: That was just hurtful.

WALTER: I have a crime lab!

FRANK: So forgive me if I don't feel real compelled to take it on faith.

BRADLEY: Frank, when are you going to accept the truth? Whether you like it or not, we live in a world of wonders. And for the first time in a long time, maybe the first time in your life, you're witnessing just that.

FRANK: A man can only believe so much.

BRADLEY: Come on. Where's the fun in that?

WALTER: Besides, if I was so duplicitous, would I cut my own hand?

FRANK: Maybe.

WALTER: Piffle. I detest the sight of blood.

FRANK: Maybe it ain't real.

(FRANK *takes* WALTER's *cut hand.* WALTER *cries out.*)

FRANK: Okay, it's real.

WALTER: That was uncalled for!

FRANK: Ah, relax. You're on the mend. Look, the blood's already dry. *(Beat)* Wait a minute. Wait one goddamn minute.

(FRANK *grabs* WALTER's *arm and examines the bandages without grabbing his hand.*)

WALTER: What on earth are you doing?

BRADLEY: Frank?

(FRANK *stares at them. The voiceover is heard.*)

FRANK: *(V O)* And just like that, the final piece fell into place.

Scene 5

FRANK: *(V O)* Like I said before, it's all about the details. Sure, it's easy to get lost in the big stuff…crazy plot-twists, shocking revelations, steamy affairs…but time and time again, it's the little things that blow a case wide open. I called them all to my office; beautiful Desiree, creepy Lyncroft, nutty Walter and old man Bradley. They all had their reasons to rub out Bernie, whether they wanted to admit it or not. But only one of 'em did it.

(Lights rise on FRANK'*s office. The four suspects are waiting alone.* BRADLEY *is talking to them.)*

BRADLEY: And once I'd learned to harness the power of Rayburnium, I knew I could make time-travel a possibility.

WALTER: My god.

DESIREE: I'm just glad to see you, wrinkles and all.

LYNCROFT: It's the worst kind of writing.

BRADLEY: Hmm?

LYNCROFT: Come now. You yourself railed against this sort of thing. The introduction of some completely implausible deus ex machina that allows the protagonist to accomplish whatever you want without any explanation needed. Science fiction rubbish.

BRADLEY: Just because you don't understand how Rayburnium works doesn't mean it's implausible. Besides, I'm standing right here!

LYNCROFT: I'm not saying I don't believe you, only that I would never have written it that way.

(The sound of a toilet flushing. FRANK *walks in.)*

DESIREE: Why are we here, Frank? Have you....?

BRADLEY: He says he's figured it out, but he wouldn't say who.

WALTER: Not til we were all together.

LYNCROFT: This seems dangerous, Mr Ellery. I'm not sure I…

FRANK: Slow down already. I know you got questions, but…look, I've been swimming in questions for the last week. I think you'll survive ten minutes in the dark.

(They quiet down. FRANK *pours a drink, then looks at* DESIREE.)

FRANK: First off, I owe you an apology.

DESIREE: Yes, I would say so. *(Beat)* Which thing are you apologizing for?

FRANK: Tossing you out 'cause of the book.

WALTER: Um…what exactly was she doing here?

FRANK: I thought you were hiding it from me. Turns out Bradley here planted it on you when you weren't looking.

DESIREE: Bradley!

BRADLEY: Come on! It's ancient history!

DESIREE: It was last week!

BRADLEY: Well, yes, from your perspective. But…

FRANK: Point is, I'm sorry. I really am.

DESIREE: It's…thank you, Frank.

*(*LYNCROFT *goes to the door.)*

WALTER: Where is he going? Where are you going?

LYNCROFT: I didn't divert my busy schedule to watch lovers reunite. If you have a point, get to it. Otherwise…

FRANK: Hold on. I gotta do something first.

*(*FRANK *takes* DESIREE's *pen and writes on a piece of paper. He puts the pen in his pocket.)*

DESIREE: What was that?

FRANK: A note to myself. I'm gonna need it later. Or yesterday. It's…anyway.

*(*FRANK *leans on his desk, looking at everyone looking at him. He laughs.)*

FRANK: My god, I'm never gonna get a chance like this again, am I?

BRADLEY: Like what?

FRANK: I mean, it's right outta Thrilling Mysteries, isn't it? The hard-boiled detective has his suspects in one room. He gets to go through the plot, slowly circling 'round to the killer, makin' the reader sweat it out til the big reveal…

WALTER: I love that part.

LYNCROFT: I know.

DESIREE: We all know. It's torturous.

FRANK: For you maybe. You've all had me dancing to separate tunes for a while. Guess what, gang. Frank's calling the shots now. *(He drinks.)* This whole thing stunk, right from the jump. Before this, you weren't nothing to me but names on stories. I wish like hell you still were, 'cause I get it now. You don't just write these worlds…you live in 'em. My life was a hell of a lot simpler before all this.

WALTER: Sounds damn boring to me.

FRANK: Maybe. But I…

WALTER: Didn't you ever want to be hero? Or a great lover? Or a mad scientist? Or a… *(He looks at LYNCROFT, can't think of a way to describe him.)* That's what we do, Frank. We don't just live in these worlds, as you say. We share them. We lift people out of the every-day, and give them a taste of the extraordinary. All for pennies-per-word.

FRANK: I'll give you that, moustache. This last week…I haven't had this much excitement since my drawing days. And yeah, it felt good to lose myself in it again. But the fact is, one of you is a killer, and it's time to pay the piper. (*He drinks again.*) A couple days ago, someone tried to kill me.

(*They all mutter surprised responses.*)

FRANK: Poison. Real nasty kind. I was almost a doornail, but Walter here saved me.

WALTER: Think nothing of it.

DESIREE: He could have poisoned you himself, then helped you to earn your trust.

WALTER: Desiree!

FRANK: It's true.

WALTER: Frank!

DESIREE: I've used that very scenario in one of my stories. (*Beat*) Not that I was the one who poisoned you.

WALTER: It was you! You poisoned your cigarettes!

DESIREE: That's nonsense!

BRADLEY: She would've been just as likely to poison herself.

LYNCROFT: Not necessarily. She could have poisoned only a single cigarette, then put that one in upside down. A casual glance could have told her which ones were safe to smoke.

BRADLEY: Good point.

DESIREE: But I didn't!

LYNCROFT: I don't make a point unless it's a good one.

DESIREE: I didn't do it!

WALTER: This is so exciting!

LYNCROFT: Although the fact that Walter was there when you needed him most…if I were reading this, it would give me pause.

DESIREE: My point exactly.

FRANK: All right…

WALTER: But I offered you my crime lab! Would I have…

DESIREE: You have a crime lab?

LYNCROFT: Of course he does.

WALTER: Oh, it's got everything. Chemical analysis, fingerprinting, a helixometer…

FRANK: Back on track!

(They fall silent. BRADLEY *has sat down, begun nodding off.)*

FRANK: So I was poisoned. That told me I was close to something, something someone was willing to kill me for. And after what had happened to Bradley, I knew it was now or never. And that's when it hit me.

WALTER: I didn't hit him!

LYNCROFT: No one said you did.

WALTER: Oh. I thought…

FRANK: I'd been playing this by your rules. Your stories, this black book and all its dirty secrets…I was so buried in the written word, I forgot to look at this like a P I. *(He removes the blood-stained handkerchief he took from Bernie's house.)* Anyone know what this is?

*(*DESIREE *raises her hand.)*

FRANK: You don't have to raise your hand.

DESIREE: It's a bloody handkerchief.

FRANK: I lifted it from Bernie's place, right out of the crime scene, in fact.

LYNCROFT: And you called me morbid.

FRANK: I didn't know why I hung on to it at first. The detective in me smelled something fishy, I guess.

WALTER: It's fish blood?

(They stare at him.)

WALTER: Go on.

FRANK: And then yesterday, I got a clue. A glimpse into the future. Didn't I, Bradley?

(They look to BRADLEY, who's asleep in a chair. He mutters in his sleep.)

BRADLEY: …gotta know when to hold 'em… *(This line can be improvised nightly.)*

FRANK: Wake him up, would ya?

(DESIREE gently wakes BRADLEY.)

BRADLEY: What? I…what?

DESIREE: Frank is about to dazzle us, sweetie.

BRADLEY: Oh. All right. *(He sits up.)*

FRANK: Brown, not red. Three little words that put humpty dumpty back together again.

LYNCROFT: What do you mean?

FRANK: It was a clue, and it got me thinking. See, funny thing about blood…when it dries, it don't stay red. It actually turns brown. Hell if I know why, but…

BRADLEY: It's the oxidation effect of the iron in the blood.

FRANK: …but it made me wonder why the blood on this hanky is still red as red could be. So I went to a buddy of mine on the force. He let me use his crime lab and…

WALTER: You used someone else's crime lab?

FRANK: I sure did, Walter.

(FRANK stares at WALTER, who backs down.)

FRANK: My buddy ran a couple quick tests. Turns out, it ain't blood on this thing at all. It's paint. Red paint. Ain't that right?

(FRANK *tosses the hanky to* LYNCROFT, *who catches it. He smiles a little.*)

LYNCROFT: It's crimson, actually.

FRANK: You're the artist. You would know.

(*The others stare at* LYNCROFT, *perhaps back off.* FRANK *goes behind his desk.*)

WALTER: Linny?

DESIREE: I told you I didn't do it.

LYNCROFT: This is flimsy evidence at best. It proves nothing.

FRANK: Yeah. You're right. (*He removes a gun from his desk, points it at* LYNCROFT.) That's why I'm gonna need your gloves.

BRADLEY: He…what did he say?

FRANK: Been a chilly March, Lyncroft. I'm betting you still have 'em on you. Know what else I'm betting? That when my pal examines them, he's gonna find acto…acatone..

WALTER: Aconite!

FRANK: That poison…he's gonna find that on your gloves. The gloves you wore when you put your hand over my mouth. Walter, be a pal and check his pockets, would ya?

WALTER: Yes. I believe I shall.

(WALTER *empties* LYNCROFT's *pockets. The strange piece of paper from the black book falls out of them.*)

DESIREE: What is that?

(WALTER *hands it to* FRANK.)

LYNCROFT: That would be a page from an ancient Sumerian manuscript. One that has been in my collection for quite some time.

FRANK: You took it off me when we were at the asylum.

LYNCROFT: Yes.

BRADLEY: That…that was in Bernie's book!

LYNCROFT: Yes. The little wretch stole it from me.

DESIREE: And…and you killed him for it?

LYNCROFT: "Sacrificed" would be the more appropriate description.

WALTER: Oh my god…

LYNCROFT: Well, Mr Ellery. It appears your show is done. May I go now?

BRADLEY: You bastard.

FRANK: Yeah, let's go right to the station. How does that sound?

LYNCROFT: I think not.

BRADLEY: You…you murdered Bernie.

LYNCROFT: There's still much to do.

BRADLEY: I'll kill you!

(BRADLEY *lunges at* LYNCROFT, *who grabs him, using him as a shield against* FRANK.)

LYNCROFT: Dear boy, it seems you've slowed a step or two since I caved your head in.

DESIREE: Don't hurt him!

FRANK: Slow down.

LYNCROFT: I should kill you now. It would be merciful compared to what is coming next. But then, where's the fun in mercy?

BRADLEY: Shoot him, Frank. Shoot him!

WALTER: Wait!

BRADLEY: I don't care if I die, just…!

(LYNCROFT covers BRADLEY's mouth.)

LYNCROFT: I'll break his neck, Mr Ellery. Old as he is, it will snap like a matchstick. Please drop your gun.

(FRANK doesn't.)

LYNCROFT: I have worked for years to write this final chapter, and I will not be stopped now. Drop. Your. Gun.

(BRADLEY cries out as LYNCROFT tightens his grip. FRANK lowers his gun.)

LYNCROFT: Thank you. I invited some friends, and they don't much care for firearms.

FRANK: What the hell are you…?

(The lights flicker. The strange, alien sound from before is heard.)

WALTER: Oh. Oh dear.

DESIREE: What is that?

LYNCROFT: My new representation.

(The sound grows louder and the lights start to flicker more. Strange shapes can be seen in the shadows. The others start to cry out amidst the sound as the lights black out. When they rise, all but LYNCROFT lie unconscious on the floor.)

LYNCROFT: I told you before, Mr Ellery. We're in my story now.

(Lights fade.)

Scene 6

(Lights rise on LYNCROFT'*s parlor. It is much more sinister, with macabre artwork and an altar.* FRANK, WALTER *and* BRADLEY *are tied to the wall.* DESIREE'*s tied to the altar, wearing a sacrificial gown. They are all unconscious.* LYNCROFT *stands behind the altar, wearing occult robes and holding a ceremonial dagger. He reads from the Sumerian page.)*

LYNCROFT: Albath olydra, zalbaran ath mith perro
Ool varia mith ma-heron shulabeth
Olva shulam, Olva pay-ram, Olva reth
Arise, Zal'n-thok, lord of the ancient world and
  guardian of the gate.
Arise, Zal'n-thok, sleeper beyond dreams, from your
  tomb beneath the earth.
The path is made clear.
The door is unbound.
Arise, and reclaim that which was once yours, and
  shall be yours again.

(A tremor shakes the room. The others awake with a start.)

FRANK: Christ, my head….

WALTER: What's going on? Where are we?

DESIREE: Frank?

FRANK: I'm here, doll. Just…

LYNCROFT: Good. I had hoped you wouldn't sleep through this.

BRADLEY: God, my arthritis…

FRANK: What the hell is this, Lyncroft?!

LYNCROFT: The end of now, the beginning of the old and the new.

BRADLEY: Oh good. Cryptic.

DESIREE: I can't move! And what am I wearing?!

WALTER: None of us can. The fiend has us trapped.

FRANK: Hey! What're you doing with Desiree?

LYNCROFT: Come now, Mr Ellery. You've drawn enough lurid covers. Do you not recognize a ritual sacrifice when you see one?

DESIREE: Oh god no!

(DESIREE *struggles, but can't break free.* LYNCROFT *gags her.)*

FRANK: Hurt her, and I swear to God…

LYNCROFT: No hollow threats, please. You're helpless, she's helpless, and the God you swear to is about to die bloody.

WALTER: You…you're a madman.

LYNCROFT: No! The doctors told me that when I was just a boy. Could a madman have achieved all this?

WALTER: You can't possibly think you're going to… what is it you think you're doing?

(LYNCROFT *holds up a very old book, places the pages inside it.)*

LYNCROFT: This tome is millennia old. My father brought it back from one of his sojourns. It became his obsession, and later mine. He mastered some small magic from within it, released a demon from a long-forgotten time. That demon possessed my mother, and killed my father. And so the book came to me.

BRADLEY: This is where you came up with all your batshit ideas for your stories.

LYNCROFT: Oh yes. It's all in here. The ancient gods, and their master…Zal'n-thok, the sleeping deity. You see, my friends…

FRANK: No! Don't you even… (*He struggles to free himself.)*

WALTER: Quiet, Frank.

FRANK: No damn speeches, you hear me?

(WALTER *stares at* FRANK *intently.*)

WALTER: I really think we should hear this. All right?

LYNCROFT: All these years of writing…I was trying to
prepare the world, make them aware that a new age
was about to be ushered in. But they…diminished it.
Turned it into tawdry tales of shock and fear, never
looking beyond the page. Oh, I may have grown
wealthy from the huddled masses, but they never
understood the truth of my message. Especially not…
the critics.

BRADLEY: Now, Lyncroft. None of us love the critics,
but…

LYNCROFT: Vile, contemptuous gasbags. The minute
something is beyond them, they blame the writer.
Never do they think that perhaps they might be at
fault, perhaps they might simply be too narrow of
vision. And yet they foist their opinions unasked,
claiming expertise and proving with every syllable that
they possess nothing of the kind.

WALTER: You've really put some thought into this.

LYNCROFT: The greatest mistake God made was
convincing those who create nothing that theirs should
be the loudest voices. I will see all critics wiped from
the face of the earth.

FRANK: But…didn't you say that everyone was a critic?

(*Another tremor*)

LYNCROFT: Now you're catching on.

BRADLEY: You can't be serious.

LYNCROFT: Deadly. With this final sacrifice, Zal'n-thok
shall awaken fully. He will ascend from the bowels

of the earth and lay waste to the world of man. Had that worm Wolcott not stolen a page from my book, it would have happened all the sooner.

BRADLEY: Is that why you attacked me? You thought I had it but…

LYNCROFT: Yes, that was unfortunate. But fortune smiled on me in the form of Frank. He followed the bread crumbs I laid and tracked down my missing page, the page that contained the final incantation necessary to revive the Ancient Ones.

FRANK: Petty theft ain't no reason to cut a man's heart out.

LYNCROFT: There was nothing petty about it. I in fact used his heart to begin this great spell. I shall complete it by removing Ms St Clair's.

(WALTER *rises, unbound.*)

WALTER: Not if the Cloak has anything to say about it.

(LYNCROFT *staggers back, grabbing his knife.*)

WALTER: Your forget, Lyncroft. I have written hundreds of scheming villains.

LYNCROFT: How did you…?

WALTER: All I had to do was get you gassing on about your plans. That bought me all the time I needed to free the lot of us.

(FRANK *and* BRADLEY *rise, realizing they are also free.*)

FRANK: The hell…?

WALTER: I spent a year learning the escapist arts from Major Zamora himself!

(LYNCROFT *raises the knife above* DESIREE.)

LYNCROFT: Then I'll simply…

FRANK: No!

(Another tremor, much stronger. They all fall.)

LYNCROFT: It has begun. Zal'n-thok opens his eyes.

FRANK: Come on, get up!

LYNCROFT: What ruled below shall now reign above.

FRANK: It's three of us against one cookoobird. We can do this!

LYNCROFT: How? I took all your weapons while you slept.

BRADLEY: Oh my god…I remember…

WALTER: What? What is it?

BRADLEY: It's…today is March 10th, isn't it?

FRANK: Now ain't the time to…

BRADLEY: Isn't it?!

FRANK: Yeah, I think so. Why…?

BRADLEY: This is the Long Beach Earthquake.

LYNCROFT: Rise, o master! Rise!

BRADLEY: It's happening, right now! This is the earthquake that took you…took all of you…and it's happening now!

(BRADLEY hobbles to LYNCROFT, who brandishes his knife.)

BRADLEY: You have to stop this!

LYNCROFT: Never!

BRADLEY: I know what happens! Whatever it is you're trying to do…it sets off an earthquake that kills thousands of people! Half the city falls into the ocean!

LYNCROFT: What do I care!? Los Angeles will only be the start!

BRADLEY: You're a madman.

LYNCROFT: I'm not mad! I'm creative!

(LYNCROFT *stabs* BRADLEY *in the stomach.*)

FRANK: Brad!

(FRANK *and* WALTER *rush to* BRADLEY.)

FRANK: Oh, Jesus. Hang in there, kid.

BRADLEY: You have to stop him.

WALTER: I will, old sport. I will.

(WALTER *rushes to* LYNCROFT.)

FRANK: Just don't close your eyes.

LYNCROFT: I hated your work most of all, Walter. So black and white, so cliché.

WALTER: Oh yes?

FRANK: Brad?

LYNCROFT: You always assumed the villain would overlook something vital and….

WALTER: Like powdered Jumba Root?

(WALTER *reaches into his suit pocket and tosses the powder into* LYNCROFT's *face. He chokes and coughs.* WALTER *grabs for the knife. They struggle.*)

FRANK: I'm sorry.

BRADLEY: No need. If you…fix everything in the past…I won't even exist. Not like this, anyway.

FRANK: What?

BRADLEY: …the future I come from…will change… maybe I'll still be alive there…and happy…

FRANK: Brad…

BRADLEY: Maybe the new future…will be full of hope… and promise…

FRANK: You're not making any sense.

BRADLEY: …that's why I never wrote…time travel…so damn hard to explain…

(BRADLEY *dies. A cloud of colored smoke rises around him. When it clears, he's gone. As they've talked,* LYNCROFT *has managed to choke* WALTER *into unconsciousness.* FRANK *rises just as* WALTER *collapses.* LYNCROFT, *still choking, looks for the fallen knife.* FRANK *stands on it.*)

FRANK: Lookin' for this?

LYNCROFT: Give that back.

FRANK: Not a chance.

LYNCROFT: I have to finish this spell! Zal'n-thok will not rise until I offer him a second heart!

FRANK: You're not makin' the case you want to make, pal.

(FRANK *picks up the knife and goes to* DESIREE. *He begins to cut her bonds.*)

LYNCROFT: No!

(LYNCROFT *rushes him. They struggle.* LYNCROFT *manages to get the knife and stabs* FRANK *in the shoulder.* FRANK *stumbles back.*)

LYNCROFT: Now lie there and watch the world's ending. I'm curious to hear an artist's opinion on it.

(LYNCROFT *raises the knife over* DESIREE. FRANK *rises, growing weak.*)

FRANK: This ain't over, Lyncroft.

LYNCROFT: Tell that to Desiree's corpse.

FRANK: I'm…gonna stop you.

(LYNCROFT *laughs loudly. The tremors return.*)

LYNCROFT: You can't be serious! I am the High Priest of Zal'n-thok, harbinger of the final days! And you… you're a bloody and broken scribbler without a weapon to your name!

FRANK: I still got one weapon left, you son of a bitch.

(FRANK *removes* DESIREE*'s pen from his pocket.* LYNCROFT *stares, confused.*)

LYNCROFT: Is that a pen?

FRANK: Want a closer look?

(FRANK *rushes him, stabbing him in the chest with the pen. He staggers back while* FRANK *starts to free* DESIREE.)

DESIREE: Oh god, thank you!

LYNCROFT: You…you killed me.

FRANK: Just relax, baby. I'm getting you out of here.

LYNCROFT: Perhaps…not how I…would have written it, but…

(FRANK *lifts* DESIREE *off the altar, stares at* LYNCROFT.)

FRANK: You know what they say. The pen is mightier than…

LYNCROFT: Stop. Please. No…clichés…

(LYNCROFT *collapses. The room shakes.*)

DESIREE: You're hurt!

FRANK: We gotta move! This whole place is coming down! (*He tries to run, but falls.*)

DESIREE: You've lost too much blood.

FRANK: Then get Walter and go. I'm just gonna…lie down…

(FRANK *collapses.* DESIREE *shakes* WALTER *into consciousness.*)

WALTER: …I am the midnight defender…

DESIREE: Wake up, Walter! We have to…

(*Another loud tremor*)

WALTER: My god! I killed Lyncroft!

DESIREE: Help me Frank! We have to…!

WALTER: I knew I had it in me! Now let's…

(A loud crash and the lights go out.)

WALTER: Oh my.

(A loud crash)

Scene 7

(Lights rise on FRANK's office. He is cleaning it a bit. The voiceover continues over the action.)

FRANK: *(V O)* You thought we didn't make it out, didn't ya? Well, remember when Desiree said "I have muscles you can't imagine?" She wasn't foolin'. She dragged me out of the rubble, though Walter swears he helped. Turns out it was an earthquake, though not as bad as Bradley predicted. Some buildings went down, including Lyncroft's. The earth swallowed him and his crazy book up, with none the wiser. I'll never know if he really was gonna end the world. What I did know was the case was solved.

(FRANK picks up some of his old illustrations, stares at them.)

FRANK: *(V O)* Walter wrote the whole damn thing into his newest story. Changed some names, wrote me out completely. *The Case of the Pulp Killer.* He tells me the C B S is gonna use it in their first broadcast of his show. As for Bradley…well, the kid is still sleepin' the deep sleep. But if what Old Man Bradley said is right, he'll wake up in a few years. I hope to hell he makes a future like he always dreamed. Something he said keeps comin' back to me. "Whether you like it or not, we live in a world of wonders." I'm getting that now. I'm finally getting it.

(FRANK starts to hang the picture on the wall.)

FRANK: *(V O)* I spent too many years in a fog. I thought that without my hands, I wasn't worth a tinker's dam. Trust me, gentle readers, that ain't no way to live a life. In a world like this one, all you have to do is scratch the surface, and you'll see things that'll break your heart and dazzle your imagination. It ain't safe, it ain't always smart, but I'll tell you this for free; it sure as hell ain't to be missed. That's how I found myself again. And all it took was one beautiful dame with a wild story to get me out my door.

(A knock on the door)

FRANK: *(V O)* Oh, you wanna know what happened to Desiree?

FRANK: Door's open.

(DESIREE walks in.)

FRANK: *(V O)* Sorry, folks. I don't kiss and tell.

DESIREE: I got us tickets.

FRANK: Tickets to what?

(DESIREE holds them out. FRANK reaches for them, and she pulls him close and kisses him. He reads the tickets.)

FRANK: *King Kong*? Hot damn!

DESIREE: Have you seen it yet?

FRANK: Nope. I was kinda busy.

DESIREE: Fair enough. Well, it just so happens that my friend Fay…she worked on the film, you know… anyway, she tells me that the director actually studied real gorillas to replicate the way they move.

FRANK: Uh-huh.

DESIREE: Now what's interesting are the robberies.

FRANK: Robberies?

DESIREE: Oh yes. Several members of the cast have had their rooms broken into, and their jewelry stolen by a… one moment… *(She pulls out a piece of paper and reads it.)* …."A large hulking man wearing what looked like a hair shirt."

(Beat)

FRANK: So…you're thinking there's a trained ape out there liftin' marbles because…what?…no one would suspect a big monkey?

DESIREE: Provocative, isn't it? Just your kind of case.

(FRANK puts his arms around DESIREE.)

FRANK: What would I do without you?

DESIREE: I shudder to think. So, a night at the movies?

FRANK: Yeah, and maybe we'll ask a few questions while we're there.

DESIREE: That's what I like to hear.

(DESIREE and FRANK kiss. He grabs his coat.)

FRANK: Think we should give Walter a call?

DESIREE: He's not coming on our date, dear.

FRANK: Nah, but maybe after. Turns out he's not the worst detective in the world.

DESIREE: Why, Frank! I believe you've made a friend!

FRANK: Eh, he grows on you. Like a fungus.

(DESIREE gives FRANK a look.)

FRANK: But a good kinda fungus.

DESIREE: You two are very cute.

FRANK: You should see his crime lab. Helluva thing.

DESIREE: I have no doubt. Now shall we…

(FRANK takes DESIREE's hand, spins her to him.)

DESIREE: OH!

FRANK: You know somethin', Ms St Clair?

DESIREE: What's that, Mr Ellery?

FRANK: I might just have to make an honest woman out of you one of these days.

(DESIREE *laughs.*)

DESIREE: Oh Frank…I'd love to see you try.

(DESIREE *and* FRANK *kiss, then walk out the door. Lights fade.*)

END OF PLAY

www.ingramcontent.com/pod-product-compliance
Lightning Source LLC
Chambersburg PA
CBHW052150090426
42741CB00010B/2212